Key stage 3

 **Oxford history study units**

JON CRESSWELL *and* PETER LAURENCE

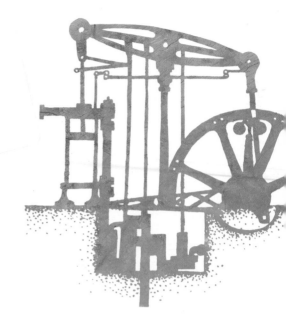

Contents

Oxford University Press 1993

Oxford University Press,
Walton Street, Oxford OX2 6DP

*Oxford New York Toronto
Delhi Bombay Calcutta Madras
Karachi Kuala Lumpur Singapore
Hong Kong Tokyo Nairobi
Dar es Salaam Cape Town
Melbourne Auckland Madrid*

and associated companies in
Berlin Ibadan

Oxford is a trademark of
Oxford University Press

© Oxford University Press 1993

ISBN 0 19 917197 1

Typeset by MS Filmsetting
Limited, Frome, Somerset.
Printed in Italy
by G. Canale & C. S.p.A. - TURIN

Preface

This book is structured as an investigation into life between the years 1750 and 1900. It focuses on the central questions: 'What changes took place between 1750 and 1900?' and 'Did these changes make life better or worse?'. These questions can be explored and answered by pupils at a variety of levels, depending on their ability.

Having established the question, the book invites pupils to put forward an initial hypothesis, using their existing ideas, assumptions or prejudices. This hypothesis can then be developed or amended as pupils work through the material. The initial hypothesis and subsequent changes can be recorded by pupils in their own books or, if they are working in groups, as part of a wall-display. A sheet for summarising conclusions is contained in Teacher's resource book 2. The conclusion to the book asks pupils to produce their final answer, which will enable them to see how far they have come in their understanding of the period.

The central questions about change and consequence were not chosen haphazardly. The focus on change, continuity, and causation means that pupils can develop their understanding of key elements of Attainment Target 1 without the need to resort to 'add on' exercises. In particular, it is hoped that pupils will discover that change can affect different people in different ways, depending on who they are, where they lived, and when they lived. Opportunities for recording pupils' work in relation to these and other Attainment Targets are provided in the exercises indicated by the headings in the chart on the right. The other British core books in this series are similarly structured around ideas of change and causation; other titles in the series give pride of place to questions linked to other Attainment Targets. Details of this, marking schemes, and homework sheets can be found in Teacher's resource book 2.

The structure of the book is thematic with the investigation being pursued chronologically within each chapter. Overall, the content of the book more than meets the demands of the National Curriculum. A wide variety of activities are used within the book, but little specific direction is given on the use of oral, written, or group work. This is a deliberate policy in order to maximise the individual teacher's freedom of choice.

Last but not least, it is hoped that the material in *Expansion, trade and industry* allows pupils to understand that these events involved real people, both famous and unknown, who like us were sometimes right and sometimes wrong, sometimes cruel and sometimes kind, and who sometimes found it easy to cope with change and sometimes could not cope at all.

Notes to teachers

Exercises offering opportunities for developing pupils' understanding of concepts and skills required in Attainment Targets are signposted as follows. Most (but not all) of the questions in these exercises are linked to Statements of Attainment. Here and throughout the book, remorseless linking of questions to Attainment Targets would have proved an intolerable burden for everyone. However, questions at the end of each chapter do open up opportunities for explicit discussion of the concepts that lie behind the Attainment Targets. Such explicit discussion is vital for the development of pupils' understanding.

AT1a	Changes		15	27	33	37	77
AT1b	Causes and Consequences		12	25	45	55	77
AT1c	People in the Past		9	20	47	53	77
AT2	Different Views			21	74	75	77
AT3	Evidence	29	42	51	63	67	77

For,
Lesley, Joseph, and John;
Becky and William

Investigating industrial Britain

In 1761, the year after George III became king, the Society for the Encouragement of Arts, Manufactures and Commerce held an exhibition in London. The Society hoped to interest people in industrial inventions. Most of the exhibits were models – a saw-mill, windmills, spinning-wheels – but there were hardly any visitors. Britain was still a farming nation – not an industrial one.

On 1 May 1851, 90 years later, George's grand-daughter, Queen Victoria, opened another exhibition organised by the Society. It was held in a huge glass building – the Crystal Palace – in Hyde Park, London, and housed over 100,000 exhibits. Most were made in Britain. The exhibition aimed to show the world how much progress had been made in British industry, science and technology. No other country could match her – Britain had become 'the Workshop of the World'. This time, millions of visitors came.

At the end of the nineteenth century Britain was still the world's leading trading nation. When Victoria celebrated her Diamond Jubilee – 60 years as Queen – in 1897, thousands of her subjects flocked to London to join the celebrations. They came from India,

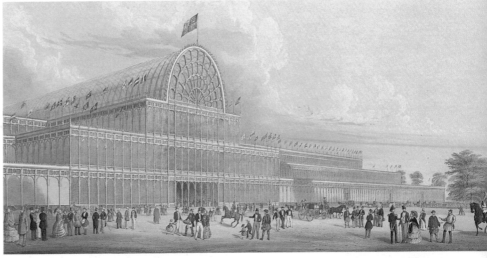

Africa, the West Indies, Canada, Australia, South-East Asia. Victoria ruled over the largest empire the world has ever seen. The Empire was defended by Britain's powerful navy. However, by 1897 other countries had begun to challenge her position.

How did Britain change between 1750 and 1900?

The pictures on the next three pages show what Britain was like in the 1750s, the 1830s and late 1890s. What changes can you observe in the three pictures? (It might help to draw up a chart. Some of the headings you could use are: Transport; Industry; Farming; Buildings. Can you think of any more?)

The 'Crystal Palace' in London's Hyde Park. Six million people visited the Great Exhibition. One woman even walked from Cornwall to see it.

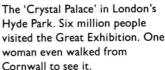

The British machinery department at the Great Exhibition

Britain in the 1750s

Britain in the 1830s

Britain in the late 1890s

Your investigation

This book is about the changes that took place in Britain between 1750 and 1900. Many of the changes were much greater, more rapid and far-reaching than the developments of the previous 700 years. Some historians have described these changes as being like a revolution – an 'Industrial Revolution'. As part of your investigation into this period of British history, you will be concentrating on two key questions.

🔍 *What changes took place?*

🔍 *Did these changes make people's lives better – or worse?*

Constructing your hypothesis

Historians study changes in the past. They try to work out what caused them, and what effects they had on people's lives. To do this, historians first examine the primary and secondary evidence about the changes they are studying. They build up an idea – or *hypothesis* – about the causes and effects of these changes. Historians then test this hypothesis by examining more evidence, and alter it if the new evidence provides more information. Historians do not always agree with each other, and often there might not be a 'right' answer to a historical problem.

When you looked at the three pictures of life in Britain, you may have thought that life looked better or worse in one picture. An idea like that is the beginning of your hypothesis. Use the information in the chart you drew up (see page 3) to answer the question below. However – be prepared to change your mind later in your work as you find out more about Britain between 1750 and 1900!

🔍 *Did people's lives become better or worse between 1750 and 1900?*

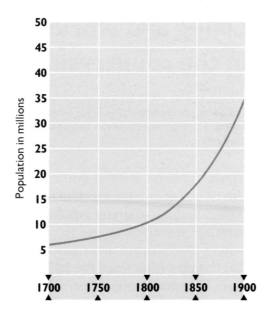

Population growth in Britain, 1700–1900

POPULATION GROWTH

One of the biggest changes that took place between 1750 and 1900 was in population size. Study the graph.

1   What was the size of the population of Great Britain in 1750?
   What was its size by 1900?
2   When did the population grow most rapidly?
3   What problems might the growth in population have caused between 1750 and 1900? You might like to consider the following areas:
   a feeding and clothing people
   b housing
   c transport
   d employment
4   Can you think of any advantages that might result from the growth of population?

Living and working in the countryside, 1750–1900

This aerial photograph shows fields enclosed by hedges. The Medieval strips can also be seen in the fields.

If you had lived in 1750 you would almost certainly have worked on the land in farming and you would have been facing major changes to your way of life. In many areas farming had changed little since the Middle Ages. The land around each village was still divided into large open fields. Local families farmed strips of land in each field.

By 1750 a major argument was underway about farming. New methods of farming were urgently needed to feed the growing population. In many areas a way of farming the land known as enclosure was being introduced. Enclosure meant breaking up the villages' open fields. These were divided into separate farms with small individual fields enclosed by fences, hedges or ditches. Today, we are used to enclosed fields but in the 1700s feelings ran so high that anti-enclosure riots took place and people were actually killed.

Despite this, the number of enclosures continued to rise after 1750 until few open fields remained. Historians still argue about whether enclosure made life better or worse for people. This chapter investigates whether life for country people improved between 1750 and 1900.

Source A

In fact, enclosure undoubtedly worked to the advantage of the richer landowners. Opposition in Parliament was only effective when it came from some considerable landowner whose interests were adversely affected.

(C. P. Hill, a historian writing in 1957)

An open field village in 1750

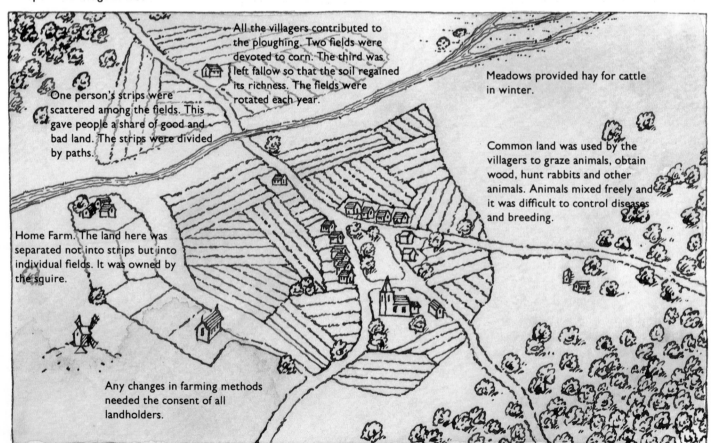

All the villagers contributed to the ploughing. Two fields were devoted to corn. The third was left fallow so that the soil regained its richness. The fields were rotated each year.

One person's strips were scattered among the fields. This gave people a share of good and bad land. The strips were divided by paths.

Meadows provided hay for cattle in winter.

Common land was used by the villagers to graze animals, obtain wood, hunt rabbits and other animals. Animals mixed freely and it was difficult to control diseases and breeding.

Home Farm. The land here was separated not into strips but into individual fields. It was owned by the squire.

Any changes in farming methods needed the consent of all landholders.

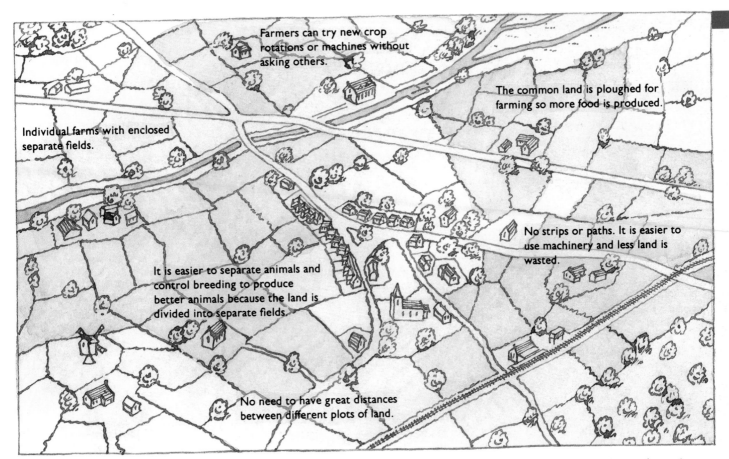

Farmers can try new crop rotations or machines without asking others.

The common land is ploughed for farming so more food is produced.

Individual farms with enclosed separate fields.

No strips or paths. It is easier to use machinery and less land is wasted.

It is easier to separate animals and control breeding to produce better animals because the land is divided into separate fields.

No need to have great distances between different plots of land.

The village after enclosure in about 1880

Source B

A more ruinous effect of this enclosure will be the almost total depopulation of their village. The poor will be driven by want of employment into manufacturing towns.

(A petition against an enclosure to the House of Commons, 1797)

Source C

Woman: Enclosure of the common land was a bad job, and ruined all us poor folk. Before it we had our garden, our bees, our share of a flock of sheep, and the feeding of our geese. And could cut turf for our fuel. Now that is gone! My cottage along with many others is pulled down and the poor are sadly put to it to get a house to put their heads in.

(A woman interviewed by Lord Torrington, *The Torrington Diaries*, 1782)

Source D

The father of the family is forced to sell his cow and his land, and being deprived of the only motive to industry, squanders the money, contracts bad habits, enlists for a soldier, and leaves his wife and children to the Parish. The poor in these Parishes may say, and with truth 'Parliament may be tender of property: all I know is that I had a cow and an Act of Parliament has taken it from me'.

(Arthur Young, *A Sixth Month Tour through the North of England*, 1770)

Source E

What were the effects of enclosures? On farming as a science, they were entirely beneficial. As land which had been waste or common land was ploughed up, the total area of cultivated land grew. Hedges helped to protect the crops from high winds, and stray animals. A greater variety of food could be produced, including more vegetables. Also, more animal fodder could be grown. This meant there was more fresh meat to be had in the winter. Enclosures were certainly a factor in enabling England to feed her growing population.

(A. J. Holland, a historian writing in 1968)

PEOPLE IN THE PAST:
ATTITUDES TO ENCLOSURES

1 Why did the open field system:
  a make it hard to introduce new ideas?
  b waste workers' time?
2 Why did the rise in population increase the demand for enclosures?
3 What arguments were used against enclosures?
4 What arguments were used in favour of enclosures?
5 Why did people disagree about whether land should be enclosed?

Enclosure

Parliament approved the enclosures if the owners of 80% of the local land wanted them. Commissioners were appointed to divide up the land, but many villagers lost out because they could provide no written proof that they owned their land.

Four-field rotation
New crop rotations were developed using turnips and ray grass. This restored the goodness of the soil without the need for a fallow field. Turnips and ray grass were used as cattle fodder so animals were not slaughtered in winter.

Large farms and long leases
Larger farms meant that improvements were easier to make. Landlords were also willing to grant longer leases to farmers keen to try out new ideas. This led to further improvement.

New machines
Such as Jethro Tull's seed drill. This was designed to plant seeds in neat rows. It replaced the old method of throwing the seeds on to the field by hand, which was slow, wasteful and made the crop difficult to weed. Although it was not very efficient it helped to inspire other new ideas.

Transport
Roads and canals made it easier to move agricultural goods to market. They also helped ideas spread because people travelled more and the postal service improved.

Manure
Large herds developed as animals were no longer slaughtered before winter. They provided more and better quality manure to enrich the soil and so more crops were produced.

Change in the countryside
This diagram shows many changes that took place in the countryside in the period 1750–1830. These changes were much easier to introduce because of enclosures. Why would each change make it easier to feed the rising population?

Banks
The development of banks provided a way for farmers to borrow money to improve their farms.

Model farms and festivals
New ideas were spread by model farms and festivals. People visited these and saw the new methods in operation.

Marl
Marl replaced the old method of digging a plant called broom into sandy soil to make it produce more crops. Marl was a mixture of clay and lime; it was more efficient and quicker acting.

Selective breeding
The best animals were separated from herds and bred to produce even better animals. These new breeds, such as the New Leicester sheep, were healthier and gave more meat than the animals which had roamed the common land.

Drainage
Land was often too wet for crops to grow. Improved drainage using ditches and clay pipes made existing land less boggy and new land was developed, increasing yields.

An animal before selective breeding

Thomas Coke 1754–1842
Coke was a landowner from Norfolk. He demonstrated the value of many new farming techniques. He granted his tenants long leases so that it was worthwhile for them to improve the land. In return he insisted they used crop rotations and marl. He also developed new methods of selective breeding. Coke held a famous agricultural show, 'Coke's Clippings', which helped the spread of new ideas.

Thomas Coke and a selectively bred animal

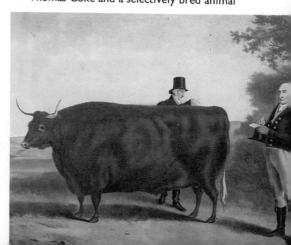

Corn Laws and Captain Swing

The changes in agriculture before 1815 helped feed the rising population but the arguments about farming continued. The wars with France (1793–1815) helped farmers because prices went up when foreign corn was hard to obtain. However, British farmers worried that when the war ended corn prices would fall and their profits would go down because cheap foreign corn would be imported.

Many Members of Parliament made money from farming and in 1815 Parliament passed the Corn Law. The Law stopped foreign corn being brought into Britain unless the price in Britain rose to a high level. This kept the price of corn high so that people still had to pay more for their bread – their staple diet. This caused great hardship for the poor.

Matters were made worse because many farmers also began to introduce new technology like threshing machines. This often meant workers were sacked or were forced to take cuts in wages to keep their jobs. In the end the high price of corn and new farming methods led farmworkers to use violence against the farmers. Some sent threatening letters, burnt barns and wrecked machinery, all in the name of Captain Swing.

Would you have rioted?

The arguments on the right are for and against the Corn Laws and the use of new ideas and machinery. Would you have joined the rioters? Explain the reasons for your choice.

Swing Rioters
The rioters used the name of Captain Swing as their leader.
This was a made up name which was designed to spread fear among landowners and avoid the real leaders being detected.

The Corn Laws and new machinery

For	Against
● We have been at war for the last 20 years. Although we are now at peace, we need to grow our own food in case war breaks out again. Without the Corn Laws cheap foreign corn will put farmers out of business. The foreign corn can be cut off at a moment's notice.	● New machines cause great unemployment and hardship and just let the rich make big profits.
● Without Corn Laws British farmers will go out of business and their workers will lose their jobs as well.	● The high price of bread hurts the poor. It also keeps wages in industry high, so the goods our factories make are more expensive and our industries grow more slowly.
● New machines are vital to help us grow enough food to feed the rising population.	● Foreigners do not make money from the sale of corn to Britain, which was stopped by the Corn Laws, so they cannot afford to buy the goods our industries make.
	● It is better for countries that grow corn cheaply to sell us their corn. We can then concentrate on what we do best – making goods in factories.

❦ The Golden Age to the Great Depression

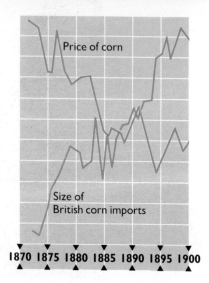

Source F

The price of corn and the size of British corn imports, 1870–1900

The Government repealed the Corn Laws in 1846 after a potato famine in Ireland. Poor harvests had led to great shortages of food. Repeal was not the disaster many farmers expected. There was no sudden flood of cheap foreign corn. In fact, the period from 1840 to 1870 is known as the Golden Age of British Farming. At this time many more new ideas were adopted to make farming more efficient and more profitable. These included better winter feeds such as linseed, better steam powered machinery and clay drainage pipes.

Widescale use was made of gangs of temporary labourers. These were often children and were employed for low pay for short periods at busy times of the year. New railways also made it easier to transport food to market. However, bad harvests and other problems meant that the Golden Age did not last. The period 1875–1895 was known as the Great Depression and farming was only just recovering by 1900. These changes affected the lives of people in many different ways.

Source G

Gang work using children. A contractor would organise a gang for a farmer to do a job for a fixed price. The contractor's profit depended on employing cheap labour, such as women and children, at low wages and making them work long hours.

Source H

Labour has been more costly, so that the average labour bill of an arable farm is at least twenty-five per cent higher than it was twenty five years ago; from the competition of other industries the labouring class has been scarcely, if at all, affected by the distress which has fallen so heavily upon owners as well as occupiers. Provisions have been cheap and abundant, while wages in a few districts only have been slightly reduced.

(1882 Commission on the state of agriculture)

Source I

a The change from rural to urban population, 1700–1901

	Urban	Rural
1700	20%	80%
1811	37%	63%
1831	44%	56%
1851	56%	44%
1901	77%	23%

b Number of farmworkers, 1850–1907

Total male farmworkers
1850 1124000
1907   674000

Total female farmworkers
1850   143000
1907   13500

CAUSES AND CONSEQUENCES: GOLDEN AGE AND DEPRESSION

1. Why were farmers' profits higher between 1840 and 1870?
2. How does Source F explain the problems facing farmers after 1870?
3. By 1870 many foreign countries had **a** refrigerated steamships, **b** railways, **c** canning factories. How did this cause problems for British farmers?
4. Not all farmers felt there was a depression. Which farmers benefited from low grain prices and had little foreign competition?
5. Who else benefited from low grain prices and the growth of grain imports?
6. What does Source H suggest happened to the wages of some farmworkers between 1870 and 1900?
7. What does Source G suggest life was like for some farmworkers and part-time farm labourers?
8. Look at Source I. Use the information on this page to explain why the rural population fell between 1750 and 1900.
9. Which of these statements do you agree with?
   Between 1750 and 1900 changes in agriculture made life
   a better for all farmers, farmworkers and their families.
   b worse for all farmers, farmworkers and their families.
   c better for some farmers, farmworkers and their families.
   Explain the reasons for your choice.

Working in industry, 1750–1900

Richard Oastler, 1789–1861. Oastler's tireless campaigning for factory reform earned him the nickname of 'The Factory King'.

Changes in agriculture such as enclosure and the use of new machinery meant that some people lost their jobs in farming. Many of them found new jobs in factories. The development of factories was one of the most important changes in the period 1750–1900. But in 1830, Richard Oastler of Huddersfield wrote the following letter to a newspaper called the *Leeds Mercury*. He described working conditions in the new factories.

Richard Oastler's letter probably represents the impression that most people nowadays have of those early factories. In this chapter you will look at some of the changes in the ways people worked between 1750 and 1900 to see whether Oastler's claims were true or false.

YORKSHIRE SLAVERY

1 Make a list of the conditions Oastler mentions.
2 What is Oastler's attitude towards the new factories?
3 Which of Oastler's statements are facts and which are opinions?

Yorkshire slavery

Let truth speak out, appalling as the statement may appear. The fact is true. Thousands of our fellow-creatures and fellow-subjects, both male and female, the miserable inhabitants of a Yorkshire town, are this very moment existing in a state of slavery, more horrid than are the victims of that hellish system, 'Colonial Slavery'. The very streets which receive the leaflets of an 'Anti-Slavery Society' are every morning wet by the tears of innocent victims who are compelled (not by the cartwhip of the negro slave driver) but by the equally appalling thong or strap of the over-looker, to hasten half-dressed, but not half-fed, to those magazines of British, infantile slavery — the worsted mills in the town and neighbourhood of Bradford! Would that I might rouse the hearts of the nation, and make every Briton swear, 'These innocents shall be free.' Thousands of little children, both male and female, but principally female, from seven to fourteen years of age, are daily compelled to labour from six o'clock in the morning to seven in the evening, with only — Britons, blush while you read it! — thirty minutes for eating and recreation.

Child labour in a textile mill.
In the early nineteenth century children were often expected to work long hours in conditions which seem terrible to many people today.

⬚ **Changes in industry, 1750–1900**

Different industries make different sorts of things: the iron industry makes iron, the textile industry makes cloth and so on. Between 1750 and 1900, the type of industry found in Britain, and the parts of the country in which the industry was found, changed.

Throughout this period the major British industries remained iron, coal and textiles. But, as the map shows, by 1900 iron and textile production had become concentrated in the coal-mining areas because they used coal as a fuel. A greater variety of industries also developed, and by 1900 new materials such as rubber, early types of plastic made from oils, and aluminium were in use. The new industries also tended to locate themselves in the areas favoured by the more established industries.

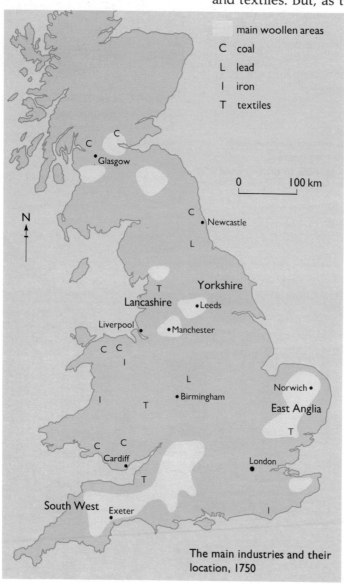

main woollen areas
C coal
L lead
I iron
T textiles

0   100 km

The main industries and their location, 1750

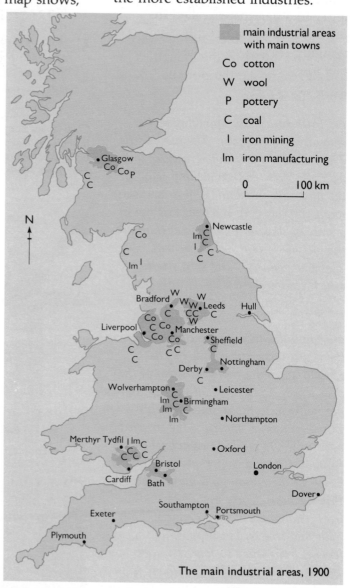

main industrial areas with main towns
Co cotton
W   wool
P   pottery
C   coal
I   iron mining
Im iron manufacturing

0   100 km

The main industrial areas, 1900

BRITISH INDUSTRY, 1750–1900

Look at the maps.
1 What were the main industries in 1750?
2 What changes were there in the location of the textile and iron industries between 1750 and 1900?
3 What were the major industrial areas in 1900? How did they differ from those in 1750?
4 What are the benefits of using new materials like rubber, plastic and aluminium?

Changes in power

In 1750, the main types of power were hand, animal and water power. As people wished to make more things, they needed better types of power to drive the machines. This would allow things to be made more quickly and easily. At first, more use was made of water power, but gradually the old types of power were replaced in many industries by steam. Steam remained the most important source of power throughout the nineteenth century, but by the 1890s some industries had begun to see the potential of gas and electricity.

A Watt steam-engine being removed in 1898 having worked for 120 years!

James Watt 1736–1819

Watt was employed by Glasgow University as a maker of scientific instruments. He was asked to repair a model steam-engine of the type used in mines. He saw it could be improved, but he only became successful when he went into partnership with the businessman, Matthew Boulton in 1774.

- They developed engines which were much more powerful.
- They developed new gears which allowed their engines to produce rotary motion, suitable for driving machinery in factories.

CHANGES: POWER

1 What were the advantages and disadvantages of
   a hand and animal power?
   b water power?
2 What were the benefits of steam power?
3 How would the use of water and steam power lead to the growth of factories?

4 Where would you expect industries to be set up if they used
   a water power?
   b steam power?
5 What are the advantages and disadvantages of gas and electricity over other types of power?
6 How might these changes affect working conditions?

Hand
In 1750 many machines were powered by hand in people's homes.

Water
Water power began to be used widely after 1750. Water was used to turn water-wheels which powered the machinery.

Animal
Some tasks in 1750 were carried out using animals.

Steam
Steam power was provided by steam-engines. Coal heated up water to make steam. The steam turned wheels linked by drive-belts to the machinery. This method was far more powerful and reliable than water power.

Gas
Gas was used to light some London streets as early as 1814. But the danger of explosions put people off until the invention of the safe gas mantle. However, the use of gas was still limited: it did not drive machines, it was still dangerous and it was not available outside major towns.

Electricity
Electric powered workshops and factories were simple and cheap. No belts were needed to drive the machinery and electric powered machines were easy to control. Before 1900 the use of electricity was limited as there was no National Grid, and different electricity companies in different cities often found it difficult to produce enough power for both industrial and domestic use.

⚙ Changes in coal mining

Richard Arkwright 1732–92

Regarded as the founder of the modern factory system, Arkwright developed other people's ideas with great success. In 1768 he designed a spinning machine called the water-frame. The water-frame could not be operated by hand; it needed the power of a water-wheel and could only be used if factories were built near streams or rivers. Arkwright set up his first mill at Cromford, near Derby, by the River Derwent which provided the source of power. More mills in Derbyshire and Lancashire followed, the largest employing 600 people. Arkwright became a millionaire and was awarded a knighthood. Others rushed to follow his example.

A family making cloth under the Domestic System.
Wealthy merchant clothiers would supply the families with wool or cotton and buy the finished cloth back from them. The cloth would then be sold at the market. Look back at the picture on page 13. Would children who were used to the Domestic System find it hard to adjust to work in the mills?

As the population grew, there were more people to buy goods. Engineers and inventors developed new machines to meet this demand. The machines made goods more quickly and cheaply but they were also much larger. Factories were needed to house the new machines powered by water-wheels and steam-engines. Pages 16–18 look at industries and how they affected the lives of ordinary people.

Textiles

In 1750, most cloth was made in people's houses. The women spun the wool or cotton into yarn or thread and the men wove the yarn into cloth. The children also helped. This system of making cloth in the home was called the Domestic System.

As the need to make more clothes grew, changes took place. The Domestic System slowly gave way to new methods, using new large machines housed in factories. The early factories used water power and were situated near to good

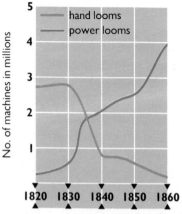

Source A

The use of steam power in the cotton industry, 1820–60
The wool industry gradually adopted the new steam-powered machines first used in the cotton industry.

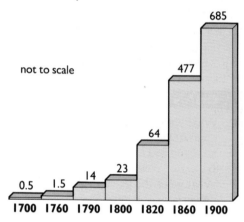

not to scale

Source B

Imports of raw cotton (in million kg)

supplies of water. Later, factories used steam and were located near to good sources of coal. Look at this evidence and begin to fill in your own copy of the chart below.

The coal industry

Between 1750 and 1900, coal was used widely in homes and factories. It was used to provide fuel for the steam-engines and on most other occasions when heat was needed. As industries like textiles used more machinery, more coal was needed. To meet this demand there had to be major changes in the way coal was mined. There were also many problems which had to be solved. Use the information opposite to add to your copy of the chart on the left.

Type of industry	What changed?	How fast was the change?	How great was the change?	How might this lead to working conditions like those on page 13?

Source C

Betty Harris, age 37: I went into a colliery when I was married and works from 6 in the morning to 6 at night. Stop about an hour at noon to eat my dinner; I get no drink. I worked when I was in the family way. I know a woman who has gone home, washed herself, taken to her bed, been delivered of a child, and gone to work again under the week. I have a belt round my waist, and a chain passing between my legs, and I go on my hands and feet. The pit is very wet where I work and the water comes over our clog tops always, and I have seen it up to my thighs. My clothes are wet through almost all day long. I am very tired when I get home at night; I fall asleep sometimes before I get washed.

(Report of the Children's Employment Commission, 1842)

Source D

Sarah Gooder, age 8: I'm a trapper in the Gawber pit. It does not tire me, but I have a trap without a light, and I'm scared. Sometimes I sing when I have a light, but not in the dark. I dare not sing then. I don't like being in the pit.

(Report of the Children's Employment Commission, 1842. Trappers were expected to open trap-doors to let the wagons of coal pass and then shut the doors to allow air currents to ventilate the mines. Children as young as five years old often did this for over 12 hours a day)

The Davy Lamp

In 1815 Humphrey Davy developed the miner's safety lamp. He wrapped a cylindrical gauze sheet around an oil lamp. The gauze stopped the flame igniting the explosive methane gases in the mines. This enabled deeper pits to be dug with less chance of explosion.

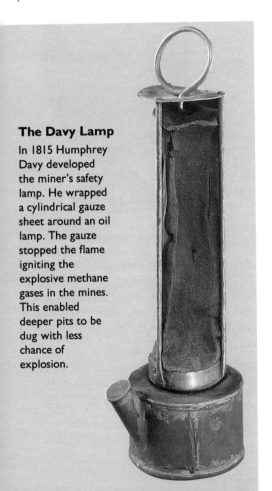

Early pits

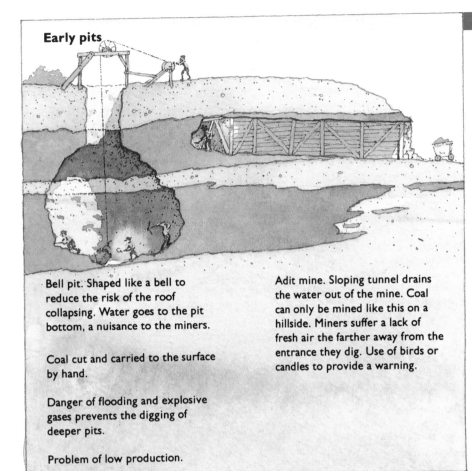

Bell pit. Shaped like a bell to reduce the risk of the roof collapsing. Water goes to the pit bottom, a nuisance to the miners.

Coal cut and carried to the surface by hand.

Danger of flooding and explosive gases prevents the digging of deeper pits.

Problem of low production.

Adit mine. Sloping tunnel drains the water out of the mine. Coal can only be mined like this on a hillside. Miners suffer a lack of fresh air the farther away from the entrance they dig. Use of birds or candles to provide a warning.

Changes in coal mining

Later pits

Deeper pits. Increased danger of flooding and explosions due to lighting and poor ventilation (methane gas creates the danger of explosions when naked flames are used).

Solutions:

a Pit props and ventilation shafts with braziers at the bottom to help air circulate.

b Trappers (small children who open ventilation doors).

c Firemen (lighted poles were used to explode dangerous gases.)

d Suction air pumps introduced after 1807.

e Davy Lamp, 1815 – a miners' safety lamp.

f Steam pumps to reduce flooding.

Mining techniques:

a New ideas only slowly introduced. Pit ponies (1763), iron rails (1767), steam railways (early 1800s), safer fuses (1830s), Wire rope and steam winches (1840s).

b Women and children banned below ground after 1842.

Engineering

Engineering grew rapidly after 1830.

Number of people employed:
Metal manufacturing, machines, implements, vehicles, precious metals

1841	410,000
1861	792,000
1881	1,026,000
1901	1,569,000

Building, construction:

1841	377,000
1861	594,000
1881	877,000
1901	1,219,000

Chemicals

The chemical industry grew rapidly after 1850 making fertiliser, dyes, soap, explosives, and other products.

Number of people employed, Chemicals, oil, soap, etc:

1841	24,000
1861	50,000
1881	81,000
1901	147,000

Soap Production:

1785	17,000 tonnes
1851	88,000 tonnes
1891	264,000 tonnes

Shipbuilding

Shipbuilding grew along the major rivers like the Tyne, the Mersey, and the Clyde and at major ports. Wooden ships gave way to iron and then to steel and the industry developed particularly quickly after 1850.

Shipping launched:

1800	50,000 tonnes
1880	660,000 tonnes

Steel

By 1870 steel could be made in large quantities. This was much stronger and more flexible than iron.

Steel production:

1850	60,000 tonnes
1870	250,000 tonnes
1880	2,000,000 tonnes
1900	5,000,000 tonnes

Other industries

Important iron and pottery industries also developed after 1750 and many other industries grew rapidly in the period 1830–1900. Look at the evidence in this section and fill in your chart.

Pottery

The pottery industry was centred on Stoke on Trent. Its growth was partly due to men like Josiah Wedgwood. The industry grew rapidly after 1800.

Number of people employed
Bricks, cement, pottery, glass

1841	58,000
1861	112,000
1881	138,000
1901	189,000

Iron

Cheap iron was vital to the growth of most industries. Once new ways had developed of separating the iron from the rock in which it was found, large iron works were built.

Iron production:

1788	61,000 tonnes
1800	200,000 tonnes
1880	7,700,000 tonnes

Abraham Darby I, II, III

Three generations of ironmasters called Abraham Darby lived and worked in Coalbrookdale in Shropshire.

- They pioneered new ways of making iron using coke, rather than charcoal, which was in short supply.
- They showed the value of steam power to power the blast furnaces.
- They used iron to make buildings and bridges.

Josiah Wedgwood 1730–95

Josiah Wedgwood rapidly expanded the Staffordshire pottery industry.

- He used adverts and salesmen to spread the news of his pottery.
- He made his works very efficient by dividing up the jobs so that each worker became skilful at a particular craft.
- He supported the Grand Trunk Canal. This helped him obtain raw materials and get goods to market more cheaply.
- He made good use of new technology such as steam-engines.

⚙ Working conditions

In the first part of this chapter you saw how industry changed between 1750 and 1900. By 1900, there is no doubt that conditions in the factories were much improved due to new laws on safety and new regulations about the age and treatment of workers.

However, the letter you read by Richard Oastler claimed that the early factories had a terrible effect on people's lives. It is now time to look in more detail at conditions in factories and test the truth of Oastler's views. You must also try to find out what working conditions were like in jobs apart from those in factories.

Source E

Elisabeth Bentley, lives in Leeds, began work at the age of six in Mr Busk's flax mill. Hours 5 a.m. till 9 p.m. when they were 'thronged', otherwise 6 a.m. to 7 at night, with 40 minutes for meal at noon.
Does your work keep you constantly on your feet?
Yes, there are so many frames and they run so quick.
Your labour is very excessive?
Yes, you have not time for anything.
Supposed you flagged a little or were too late?
What would they do?
Strap us.
Have you been strapped?
Yes, severely.
Were the girls so struck so as to leave marks on their skin?
Yes they have black marks many a time, and their parents dare not come to him about it, they were afraid of losing [the child's] work.
In what part of the mill did you work?
In the card room, it was so dusty, the dust got upon my lungs, and the work was so hard.
You dragged the baskets?
Yes, it was a great basket that stood higher than this table, that was full of weights, and pulling the basket pulled my shoulder out of its place, and my ribs have grown over it.
You are considerably deformed in consequence of this labour?
Yes, I am.

(Committee on Factory Childrens' Labour, 1831–1832)

Source F

A child, not ten years of age, having been late at the factory one morning, had, as a punishment, a rope put round its neck, to which a weight of twenty pounds [10 kg] was attached; and thus burdened like a galley slave, it was compelled to labour for a length of time in an impure atmosphere and a heated room.

(Extract from a speech by Mr Grant, a Lancashire spinner, reported in the *Manchester Courier*, 1833)

Source G

Drowsy and exhausted, the poor creatures fall too often among the machinery, which is not in many instances sufficiently sheathed; when their muscles are lacerated, their bones broken or their limbs torn off, in which case if crippled for life, they are turned out. To keep the children awake and to stimulate their exertions, children are beaten with thongs.

(M. T. Sadler; speech to the House of Commons, 1832. Sadler was a leading campaigner for better working conditions)

Source H

Mr T. Ashton employs 1500 work-people of both sexes. The young women are well and decently clothed. A sort of large apron protects their outer garments from dirt. The houses inhabited by the work-people form long and large streets. Mr Ashton has built three hundred of them which he lets at 3s or 3s 6d [15p or 17.5p] per week. The proprietor furnishes, at his own charge, water to the premises, keeps them in good repair and pays the local rates.

(Leon Faucher, a Frenchman who visited Manchester briefly in 1844)

Source I

So much nonsense has been uttered about the deformities and diseases of factory children, that I may hardly be credited by some of my readers when I assert that I have never seen so many pleasing countenances and handsome figures as I saw at Mr Ashton's weaving factories at Hyde. Their light labour and erect posture in tending the looms opens their chest, and gives them a graceful carriage. One of them, whose cheeks had a fine, rosy hue, being asked how long she had been at factory work, said nine years.

(Dr Andrew Ure, *The Philosophy of Manufactures*, 1835. Ure was a Professor of Chemistry from Glasgow. He believed that scientific methods of production were the best)

Source J

Chimney sweep and boy in 1877. Apart from factories, a common job for children was sweeping chimneys. The children were forced to climb up inside the chimneys to brush out the soot which collected there. Sometimes they would get stuck or fall.

Source K

Parents are compelled by sheer necessity to send their children to work; they could not otherwise support them; if the children were excluded from the factories and workshops it is not clear what would become of them. There is no legal provision for compelling them to attend schools, their only resource would be the street, with all its perils and temptations. We would rather see boys and girls earning the means of support in a mill than starving by the roadside.

(W. Cooke Taylor, *Factories and the Factory System*, 1844)

Source M

Boy, aged 12; works at nails; has worked at it above a year and a half, and gets from 3s 6d to 4s [17.5p to 20p] a week. His mother takes the nails he makes into the warehouse, and gets the money. Some of the boys are not well treated by their masters; they don't get enough victuals and some are beat.

Knows a boy that made scrags (bad nails), and somebody in the warehouse took him and put his head down on an iron counter and hammered a nail through one ear, and the boy made good nails ever since.

(Report by R. H. Franks for Parliament, 1843)

Source N

Sarah Griffiths, age 12. Works in the brick-yards; works under one of the men; the man never beats her; was never beaten by anybody; nobody sees that any of the girls get beaten except when they don't behave themselves, and won't do their work, and run away to play, when they don't like work, and then the men smack 'em with their hands – only on their faces and backs – not badly; thinks it's only when the girls deserve it. Works from 6 in the morning to 8 or 9 at night. Is sometimes very tired at night; has to carry very heavy weights, bricks or clay; 4 or 5 or 6 bricks at a time, as many as each one can; the girls sometimes fall down with them or drop 'em or spoil 'em, and have to bring them back; then they get smacked or turned off from the work. Finds her legs swell sometimes from running about and has pains and aches between the shoulders, and her hands swell; all this goes off when they get used to it. Can read, not write. (N.B. Growth appearing somewhat stunted, health good, clean and well clothed.)

(From R. H. Horne's Report for Parliament, 1843)

Source L

An illustration of child labour in the mines, from a report which led to the 1842 Coal Mines Act

Source O

Child matchbox makers in the late nineteenth century. In many industries children continued to be employed in the home or in small workshops throughout the nineteenth century. Their working conditions were often poor and contact with substances like glue and other chemicals sometimes caused major health problems.

Source P

1833 Factory Act

Children aged 10 to 13 are to work a maximum of 48 hours a week.
Children aged between 13 and 18 are to work a maximum of 69 hours a week.
Children are to receive 2 hours of education a day during working hours.
Four Factory Inspectors are appointed to enforce the Law.

1842 Mines Act

Women and all children under 10 years of age are not to work underground.
Inspectors are to enforce the Law.

PEOPLE IN THE PAST: WORKING CONDITIONS

1　Which sources agree with Oastler?
2　Which sources disagree with Oastler?
3　Why do you think people had different opinions about working conditions?
4　Use a selection of the sources to write an account of nineteenth-century working conditions from the point of view of
   a　a worker,
   b　an employer.
Would all people in each category agree with your account?

Working conditions: The verdict of historians

In this chapter you have seen how working conditions changed after 1750 to keep up with changes in technology. In many industries, production moved from the home to factories. Children and adults worked long hours but there was nothing new in this. What was different were the factory conditions. Although laws set minimum ages for workers, child labour remained common throughout the 1800s. You have also seen that there was a lot of argument as to how bad working conditions actually were in the 1800s.

Source Q provides a modern summary of working conditions for children in the period 1750 to 1833.

Source Q

Hours were not regular in the Domestic System. Children were exploited, working long hours. Their parents were severe task-masters and they set them to work almost as soon as they could walk. The early factories offered much better wages than could be earned on the land, but the first generation of factory workers had to get used to a new way of life. Few employers showed much concern for the welfare of their workers; they had no wish to reduce their profits, and they had struck a bargain with their workers when they had taken them on and saw no reason to modify it. It is easy to blame the employers; but remember they, too, were in a totally new situation. Who had assumed responsibility for the workers' welfare under the Domestic System? No one in particular.

Conditions were worse in the small mills (the vast majority) where the employer, concerned for profit margins, was not inclined to indulge in any sentimental interest in the conditions of his workers. Severe discipline, enforced by beatings or dismissals or fines, added to the long hours and risks of industrial injuries and diseases. The most dangerous thing in textile mills was the driving belt. If you were caught by it, you would be hurled several times against the ceiling and floor. But there were good employers, even among small factory owners. There is so much evidence of bad conditions that it is easy to exaggerate them.

(R. B. Jones, a historian writing in 1971)

Source R

Later working conditions. Clearly, by 1900 better factory regulations meant working conditions had improved for many people. But, between 1750 and 1900, did they get worse before they got better?

DIFFERENT VIEWS: WORKING CONDITIONS – BETTER OR WORSE?

1 What is Jones' answer to the question 'Did working conditions get better or worse in the nineteenth century?'
2 How would the answer be different if his only sources were
   a reports made by factory reformers?
   b factory owners' reports?
3 Films and books usually show only awful working conditions in nineteenth-century factories. Do you think that this gives a fair account of the past?
4 How might the political views or family background of a historian affect his or her answer to the question 'Did nineteenth-century working conditions get better or worse?'
5 Write your own account answering the question 'Did nineteenth-century working conditions get better or worse?'
6 Compare your account with someone else's.
   a List the agreements and disagreements.
   b Explain why they agree or disagree.

Empire, trade, and seapower

The changes that took place in industry and working conditions between 1750 and 1900 could only happen because British trade with other countries grew during this period. For example, the growth of the cotton industry depended on trade. Cotton cannot be grown in Britain, and has to be imported from abroad. Because Britain was able to manufacture cotton cloth more successfully and efficiently than other countries, she was also able to export it. In this chapter, you will be investigating how Britain's trade grew after 1750, and whether people benefited.

The British Empire in 1750
(the pink shaded areas), and goods Britain imported

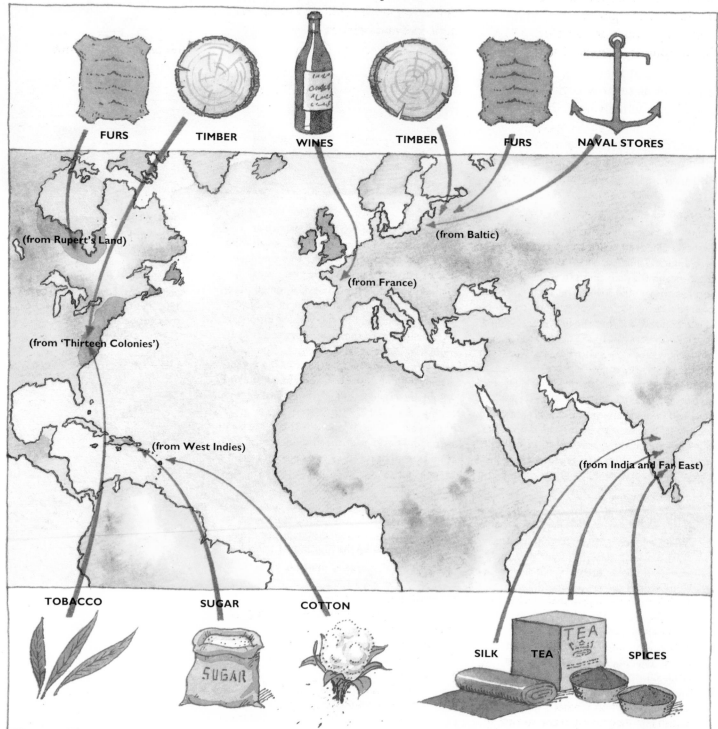

FURS   TIMBER   WINES   TIMBER   FURS   NAVAL STORES

(from Rupert's Land)

(from Baltic)

(from France)

(from 'Thirteen Colonies')

(from West Indies)

(from India and Far East)

TOBACCO   SUGAR   COTTON   SILK   TEA   SPICES

The importance of empire

One reason why Britain's trade grew after 1750 was because she gained control over many different parts of the world, and built up a huge empire. The Empire provided valuable raw materials, which Britain could import cheaply. These could either be used to produce manufactured goods for sale abroad, or could be re-exported to other countries — at a profit.

In the century or so before 1750, Britain fought a series of wars against other European countries including France, Spain and Holland. These wars were usually caused by problems and rivalries in Europe. However, much of the fighting took place overseas, where it was possible to conquer enemy colonies and gain control of their economic resources. In addition, Britain already controlled territory which had been claimed and colonised by explorers and settlers.

The British Empire in 1900

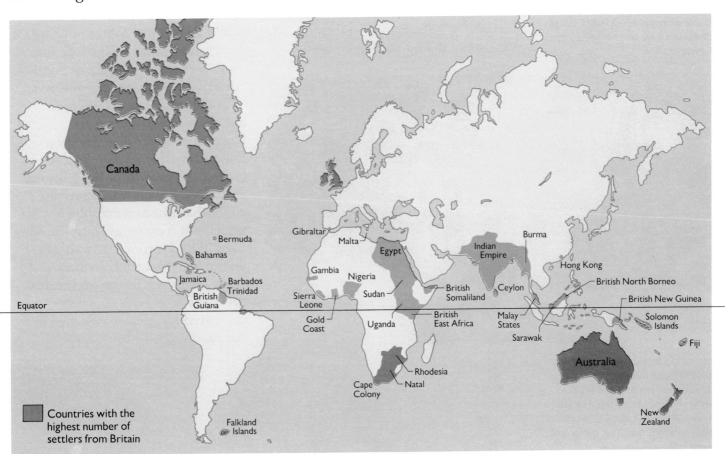

Countries with the highest number of settlers from Britain

THE GROWTH OF EMPIRE, 1750–1900

1   Compare the two maps of the British Empire.
    a   What changes took place between 1750 and 1900?
    b   What stayed the same?
2   Britain lost control of an important part of her empire between 1750 and 1900. Which part?
3   From your knowledge of geography, can you suggest any reasons why more British people emigrated and settled in certain parts of the Empire (such as Australia) and not others (such as India)?
4   How useful are these maps in explaining why the British Empire grew during this period?
5   Do you think the growth of the British Empire was likely to improve or worsen:
        the lives of people in Britain?
        the lives of the people in the British Empire?

George Washington.
Washington led the American colonists against Britain. Despite the loss of the colonies, British trade with the new United States of America actually increased after independence.

War and seapower

Between 1750 and 1815, Britain became involved in a number of European and colonial wars. The main reasons for entering these wars were to prevent other European powers from becoming too strong, and to protect British trade.

Britain versus France

France was Britain's main European and colonial rival after 1750. Canada was taken from France by the British after the Seven Years' War (1756–63), as were French trading posts in India. France gained revenge during the American Revolution (1775–83), when she helped 'The Thirteen Colonies' gain independence from Britain.

The greatest struggle between Britain and France followed the French Revolution. Between 1793 and 1815, the two countries were locked in combat, particularly after the rise of Napoleon, who hoped to extend French influence throughout the world. After Nelson's victory at the Battle of Trafalgar (1805), the French navy could no longer pose a threat to Britain, and Napoleon was finally defeated at Waterloo in 1815. As a result, Britain gained Ceylon (now Sri Lanka) and part of South Africa from France's ally, Holland.

Britain and France were not always enemies. During the Crimean War of 1854–56, they fought together against Russia, fearing the growth of her influence in Turkey. Britain was especially afraid that Russia would disrupt her trade with India or even try to take over India. However, towards the end of the nineteenth century, rivalry between Britain and France grew again, as both countries competed for greater influence in Africa.

British trade and growing wealth depended on the use of slave labour. Millions of black Africans were shipped across the Atlantic in appalling conditions to work on plantations in the West Indies and American colonies.

French cavalry charge a British infantry square at the battle of Waterloo, 1815

Colonisation and conquest

Not all British colonies were acquired through warfare with other European powers. Captain James Cook claimed Australia and New Zealand for Britain in 1770, on the grounds that he was the first European to explore their coastlines. At first, however, the British government regarded Australia as a place to send convicts. British people only began to emigrate there in larger numbers after 1830.

Many parts of the Empire were conquered to help British trade. Britain took over control of Hong Kong in 1842, following a war in which the Chinese were forced to accept opium (obtained from British India) as payment for Chinese goods, such as tea, porcelain and silk. In 1882, the British occupied Egypt, to make sure that they controlled the Suez Canal. The Canal cut the journey from India to Britain by 6500 kilometres, and was a major boost to Britain's trade.

The growth of the navy

To protect and extend her empire, Britain's navy grew considerably after 1750. The government tried to make sure that the Royal Navy was always as big as the combined navies of her main rivals. Following the Battle of Trafalgar in 1805, British naval strength was never seriously challenged until the growth of the German navy after 1900. Worldwide naval bases, like Gibraltar and the Falkland Islands, made it possible to defend trade routes successfully.

Trade and conquest were not the only motives behind British expansion. Spreading Christianity was another. Many men and women became involved in missionary work in the colonies.

Britain's fighting ships changed considerably between the 'ships of the line' which fought at Trafalgar in 1805 (left) and 'ironclads' of the late nineteenth century (below)

CAUSES AND CONSEQUENCES: WHY DID THE EMPIRE GROW?

1 Why did the British Empire grow between 1750 and 1900?

2 In what ways do you think the possession of a large empire and a large navy helped British trade?

⑩ Trade

Source A

'Plum Pottage' was a popular Christmas pudding in the eighteenth century. Here are the ingredients needed to make it:

shin of beef
water
fresh white breadcrumbs
mixed dried fruit (currants, raisins, dates, dried prunes)
grated nutmeg
ground mace
ground cloves
cinammon
salt
sherry
port
orange or lemon

The possession of an empire helped Britain's trade. You are now going to investigate how Britain's trade with other countries changed and developed during this period. To answer these questions, you will need to study the information on the maps and diagrams very carefully.

Source B

Much British trade in 1750 was centred on the North Atlantic. Slaves from West Africa had to endure the horrors of the 'Middle Passage'.

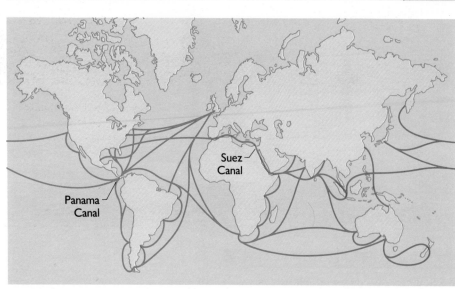

Source C

By 1900 British trade routes circled the globe

Source D

The chart shows which goods Britain imported and exported in 1750

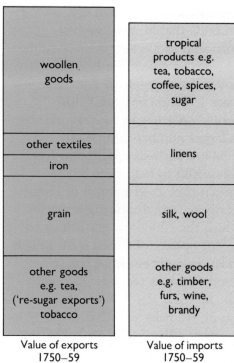

Value of exports 1750–59 £8.7 million

Value of imports 1750–59 £8.3 million

Source E

The chart shows which goods Britain imported and exported by 1900

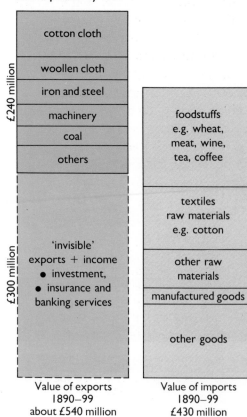

Value of exports 1890–99 about £540 million

Value of imports 1890–99 £430 million

This (stuffed!) Indian elephant aroused considerable interest at the Great Exhibition

The influence of India

Britain did not just import foreign goods. As her empire grew, and more people travelled abroad, there was a growing influence of foreign ideas, particularly from India, on British life. Curry recipes appeared in England in the eighteenth century, as did mulligatawny (a Tamil word for 'pepper-water') soup. Indian designs influenced art and architecture, and the Indian section at the Great Exhibition of 1851 attracted much admiration. Polo, snooker and billiards were games which were played by British soldiers in India, and were 'exported' to Britain. Even more importantly, India was vital to British trade. India bought huge quantities of cotton goods and other products. India was so important that she was called 'the jewel in Britain's imperial crown'.

The Brighton Pavilion was built in the 'Hindoo' style in the early nineteenth century

CHANGES: BRITISH TRADE, 1750–1900

1 Which of the ingredients in Source A do you think would have to be imported from other countries?
2 Why do we sometimes buy foreign goods rather than British ones?
3 What problems might be caused if Britain imports too many foreign goods?
4 Draw a chart to compare Britain's exports and imports in 1750 and 1900. Set your work out like this:

5 Look at your chart. Write your own description, comparing Britain's trade in 1750 with trade in 1900.

1750		1900	
Imports	Exports	Imports	Exports

Adam Smith (1723–90), the founder of the modern study of economics. His 'Enquiry into the Nature and Causes of the Wealth of Nations', (1776) put forward his beliefs that governments should interfere as little as possible in economic affairs.

Problems with trade: mercantilism, free trade and protection

Britain's large empire helped her to become wealthier through trade. Britain regarded her empire as her own property, and tried to keep foreign traders out. During the eighteenth century, trade was controlled by 'Navigation Acts', laws which said that:

- all trade to and from British colonies had to be carried in British ships;
- British colonies were prevented from sending goods such as sugar and cotton to countries outside the Empire;
- British colonies had to import all manufactured goods via Britain.

This system of controlling trade was called mercantilism. Most trading countries had similar mercantilist policies to Britain. This made it harder for Britain to export, even when she was able to produce manufactured goods, like cotton cloth and steam-engines, more cheaply than other countries. Adam Smith, a Scottish economist, called for free trade. He argued that it was natural for each country to export goods it could produce most cheaply, and to import goods which could be produced more cheaply elsewhere.

Source F

The tailor does not attempt to make his own shoes, but buys them from the shoemaker. The shoemaker does not attempt to make his own clothes, but employs a tailor. What is common sense in the conduct of every private family can scarce be folly in that of a great kingdom.

(Adam Smith, *The Wealth of Nations*, 1776)

Smugglers landing a cargo. Taxes on imports made smuggling a profitable business. Brandy, rum, wines and tea were the most common smuggled goods.

MERCANTILISM AND FREE TRADE

1   What were the advantages of mercantilism?
2   Can you see any disadvantages in mercantilism?
3   Look at Source F. What point do you think Adam Smith is making?
4   Can you see any disadvantages in free trade?

Free trade and protection

In the early nineteenth century, most countries, including Britain, taxed imports and exports. Many British manufacturers and merchants believed that these taxes restricted their ability to sell more goods abroad: other countries could not produce manufactured goods as cheaply as Britain. By 1850, almost all restrictions on foreign trade had been abandoned, and British goods could be exported freely. Although Britain still imported foreign goods, these tended to be raw materials (which were used to make manufactured articles which could be sold abroad at a profit), or foodstuffs which could not be grown in Britain.

By the 1870s, however, Germany and the United States were beginning to catch up with British industry, particularly in steel production, engineering and chemicals. In addition, cheap food was now available from abroad — wheat from North America, lamb from New Zealand and Australia, and beef from Argentina. By 1900, Britain was importing more goods than she was exporting, and her share of world trade was falling.

Some politicians demanded an end to free trade, and a return to 'protectionist' policies — placing high tariffs (taxes) on imported goods, to protect British industry from foreign competition.

Source G
'The British Lion in 1850: Or, the effects of Free Trade'

John Bull — 'I say this is getting serious'.

Source H

A cartoon from the beginning of the twentieth century about the effects of free trade

Source I

You stuff paper into the fire and reflect that the poker in your hand was forged in Germany. As you rise from the hearthrug you knock over an ornament on your mantel-piece; picking up the pieces you read, on the bit that formed the base, 'Manufactured in Germany'. And you jot your dismal reflections down with a pencil that was made in Germany.

(Taken from a pamphlet produced by opponents of free trade, 1896)

EVIDENCE: FREE TRADE AND PROTECTION

1 Does Source G suggest free trade benefited Britain or not? Explain your answer.

2 Study Source H. Does it suggest free trade benefited Britain or not? Explain your answer.

3 Study Source I. Which of the cartoons would the writer of Source I have felt best showed the effects of free trade? Explain your answer.

4 Many farmers and industrialists were badly hit by the availability of cheap foreign food and manufactured goods. Which groups of people might have benefited from them?

5 Which do you think are the most useful types of source for the study of free trade and protection – cartoons or written sources? Explain your answer.

6 What questions would you need to ask about these sources in order to decide if they were reliable or not?

7 If sources are unreliable, can they still be useful to historians?

Source J

1750–59

Total value of imports into
Britain   £8·3 million
Total value of exports from
Britain   £8·7 million

1890–99

Total value of imports into
Britain   £430 million
Total value of exports from
Britain   £540 million

Source K

Wheat prices in kilograms
1800   32p
1900   11p

**Imports of wheat and flour in
thousands of tonnes**
1800–09   101
1880–89   5209

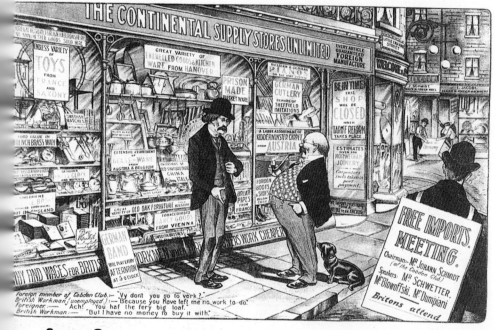

Source O

Many foreign imports, particularly
from Germany, were cheaper than
British goods. Not everyone
benefited, however, as this anti-
Free Trade cartoon suggests.

⦿ The benefits of trade

You have seen how British trade
grew and changed between 1750
and 1900, and how the possession
of a large empire helped this to
happen. Did these changes make
people's lives better or worse? To
answer this question, you need to
study the following sources.

Source L

Eggs and other dairy products, as well as
delicate fruits and vegetables, proved to
respond well to chilling once the packers and
shippers had discovered the conditions best
suited to each individual foodstuff. Swift refrigerated transport and improved canning
techniques introduced tropical and subtropi-
cal delicacies to regions which had never
known them before.

(Reay Tannahill, *Food in History*, 1975)

In 1880, the first cargo of
refrigerated beef arrived in London
from Australia; canned food was
already widely available.

Source M

British tea, sugar and tobacco consumption, in
pounds per head, in 1800 and 1900

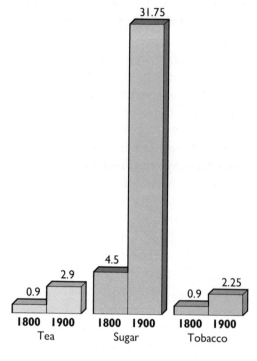

Source N

By the early 20th century, Britain continued
to sell more textiles, iron, steel and coal than
she had ever done before. But as other
countries industrialised, they excluded Britain from their markets and she had to rely
more and more on sales to less-developed
countries. Britain also failed to get a large
share of world trade in new industries:
chemical and electrical engineering, motor
cars.

(Christopher Culpin, *Making Modern Britain*,
1987)

THE BENEFITS OF TRADE

1   Study Source J. Did Britain become
wealthier through trade between 1750
and 1900? Explain your answer.

2   Study Source K.
   a   What conclusions can you come to
about the changing price of bread
between 1800 and 1900?
   b   Why do you think this happened?
   c   Who would benefit from this?

3   Study Sources L and M. In what ways
did ordinary people's lives benefit from
trade during this period?

4   The sources can only show some of the
changes in British trade during this
period. Different groups of people
were affected in different ways at
different times. From the evidence here
(particularly Sources L, N and O), how
do you think the changes in trade
affected:
   a   British farmers?
   b   British manufacturers?

5   'Everyone in Britain benefited from the
expansion of trade.' How far do you
agree with this statement?

Communications

In this chapter you are going to investigate the changes in communications between 1750 and 1900 and the effects they had on people's lives. Communications are the road, rail, sea and air routes that allow people and goods to move around the country and overseas. They are also the way ideas are carried from place to place such as by post or on the telephone.

The following statements give different views of the importance of communications. Which do you agree with?

- Good communications are very important to people's lives.
- Good communications are quite important to people's lives.
- Good communications are not very important to people's lives.

In 1750 British communications were very poor. The main methods of moving goods and people around were by road, sea or river, but many places could not be reached by river.

COMMUNICATIONS IN 1750

1 How do Sources C and D show how goods and people were moved around?
2 What was the average speed of the coach between London and Leeds and London and Edinburgh in Source B?
3 What problems faced the road traveller in 1750?
4 Why do you think heavy goods were moved by river or sea wherever possible?
5 What might have been the problems with river and sea transport?
6 Why would agriculture and industry suffer because of poor communications?

Source D

Dick Turpin holding up a stagecoach. Highwaymen like Turpin were a constant threat to travellers in the eighteenth century. Coaches that operated in the 1750s had to be built to stand up to the terrible road conditions rather than for speed or comfort.

Source A

I know not in the whole range of language to describe this damned road. Let me warn all travellers who may decide to travel through [the North of England] to avoid it as they would the devil. For a thousand to one, they will break their necks or limbs by over-throwing or breaking down. They will meet here with ruts which I actually measured four feet [1.2 m] deep and floating with mud after a wet summer. What can it be like after winter? The only mending the road gets is the tumbling in of some loose stones which serve no other purpose than to jolt the carriage around in the most intolerable manner. I actually passed three carts broken down in these 18 miles [29 km] of ghastly memory. A more dreadful journey cannot be imagined.

(Arthur Young, *A Tour Through the North of England*, 1771)

Source B

Journey times of coaches in the mid-eighteenth century
London to Edinburgh – 11 days (608 km)
London to Leeds – 4½ days (304 km)
London to Manchester – 4 days (298 km)
London to Brighton – 1 day (84 km)
London to Newcastle – 6 days (441 km)
London to Oxford – 2 days (92 km)

Source C

A packhorse convoy carrying bread to London in 1840

≋ Road improvements

To improve communications Parliament let people set up turnpike trusts. These trusts were private companies which took over local roads and charged people to use them. In return the trusts were expected to repair and improve their roads. Some even employed expert road engineers to do this.

The most famous engineers were Blind Jack Metcalfe, Thomas Telford and John Macadam (see notes on each).

Source E

Kensington Turnpike in 1820, showing road menders, the toll house and gate, and the toll collector.

Source F

Turnpikes or toll-bars have been set up on the great roads of England beginning at London and proceeding through almost all those dirty deep roads, in the Midland counties especially. At these turnpikes, all carriages, droves of cattle and travellers are obliged to pay a toll. That is to say, a horse a penny, a coach three pence, a cart four pence, a wagon six pence [six pence = 2.5p]. Cattle pay by the score or by the head. The benefits of a good road more than makes up for the small charge that travellers have to pay. Even the cost of transport of goods is reduced.

(Daniel Defoe, 1724)

Source G

1838 turnpiked and unturnpiked roads
Kilometres of turnpiked road – 35,000
Kilometres of unturnpiked road – 167,000
Typical journey time on some unturnpiked roads – 39 kilometres in 8 hours

Riots against turnpikes took place in many areas. Local people objected to the high tolls as the turnpikes made little difference to their short journeys. This picture shows a bridge being freed of tolls, 1873.

Blind Jack Metcalfe
1717–1810

Despite being blind, Metcalfe ran a successful carrier firm and built over 480 kilometres of road in the North. His roads had good stone foundations, drainage ditches, and a camber or rounded surface to allow rainwater to drain off. He developed successful methods of building roads across marshes by floating them on heather.

Source H

The ride from Leicester to Northampton I shall never forget. The getting up alone was at risk to one's life. When I was up, I was obliged to sit just at the corner of the coach with nothing to hold by but a little sort of handle. At the moment we set off, I fancied that I saw certain death ahead of me. Every moment we seemed to fly into the air, so that it was a miracle we stuck to the coach. At last being in fear of my life, I crept from the top of the coach and got snug into the basket among the trunks. When we came to go downhill, all the trunks seemed to dance around me and everything seemed to be alive. Badly bruised, I crept to the top of the coach and took my former seat. From Harborough to Northampton I had a most dreadful journey. It rained without stopping and as before we were covered in dust, now we were soaked with rain.

(Carl Moritz, writing in the late eighteenth century about a journey on a turnpike road)

Source I

Better road surfaces reduced the cost of carrying goods. Horses could carry heavier loads at higher speeds and cattle could be driven to market quicker yet arrive in better condition. But turnpikes had their short-comings too. Even after road improvements it was still costly to send freight by stage-wagon. Manufacturers continued to prefer water transport. For example, a Shropshire company in 1775 sent pig iron more than 400 miles [640 km] by sea and river to avoid a 60 mile [96 km] journey overland.

R. J. Cootes, *Britain Since 1700*, 1968)

Source J

The vehicle itself: the harness all so complete and so neatly arranged, so strong and neat and good. The beautiful horses impatient to be off. The inside full and the outside covered in every part with men, women and children, boxes, bags, bundles. The coachman taking his reins in one hand and the whip in the other gives a signal with his foot and away they go at a speed of seven miles [11 km] per hour. One of these coaches coming in, after a long journey, is a sight not less interesting. The horses are all sweat and foam, the reek from their bodies ascending like a cloud. The whole equipage is covered with dust and dirt. But it still comes in, as regular as a hand of a clock.

(William Cobbett, writing in 1818, describes the scene at a coaching inn)

Source K

Turnpikes led to major improvements in journey times. Compare the journey times for 1830 with those for the mid-eighteenth century in Source B on page 31.

Journey times 1830

London to Newcastle – 1 day
London to Edinburgh – 2 days
London to Oxford – 6 hours
London to Brighton – 5 hours

As roads improved, new faster coaches could be built. After 1784 some passenger coaches were also used to carry the mail. These mail coaches were the fastest on the road and carried armed guards to protect them. By delivering letters quickly they did much to help industry grow.

Thomas Telford 1757–1834

Telford built canals and bridges as well as roads. His roads were built to the highest standard. They had excellent foundations of large stones, good drainage, few gradients, few sharp bends. His greatest achievement was the London to Holyhead road which even included a stretch of dual carriageway across the Menai Strait Suspension Bridge. The main problem with Telford's roads was that they were very costly.

John Loudon Macadam 1756–1836

Macadam believed that roads did not require solid stone foundations. Instead he used beaten earth with a shallow layer of small stone chips which were crushed into a hard surface by the weight of traffic. This effective, cheap, method proved very popular with turnpike companies. Macadam also helped draw up a law which let all parishes raise a tax to improve local roads; this was of vital importance.

The coach on the right is the Bath Marl in 1834. Coaches often competed so fiercely to achieve the fastest times, they sometimes forced each other off the roads.

CHANGES:
ROAD IMPROVEMENTS

1 Use Source F and the picture next to it to explain how a turnpike worked.
2 If you had owned a turnpike which road engineer would you have used? Explain your answer. Remember, you want to make a profit as well as maintain the roads.
3 Did turnpikes make
   a all travel quicker and more comfortable?
   b some travel quicker and more comfortable?
   c little difference to the speed and quality of travel?
   Explain your answer.
4 What was the effect of turnpikes on freight transport?

⊞ Canals

James Brindley 1716–72

Brindley was not well educated but he soon developed a reputation as a talented engineer. He was employed by the Duke of Bridgwater to build a canal from his coalmines at Worsley to Manchester, a distance of 18 kilometres; this was completed in 1761. Brindley

● showed the value of canals because the new canal halved transport costs and also reduced flooding in the Duke's mines.
● overcame key problems of canal building by stopping seepage, using puddled clay, and crossing the River Irwell with an aqueduct. Brindley went on to construct many other canals.

Road improvements helped the movement of people around the country but it was still difficult and costly to move heavy goods over long distances. Rivers and the sea were still used to carry goods like coal and iron ore, but not all areas were close to the coast or a navigable river. Even some navigable rivers had strong currents and poor tow-paths for horse-drawn barges. For this reason businessmen began to build canals. Canals were so much cheaper for carrying heavy goods that by 1830 there were 6400 km of canals in Britain, and most parts of England and Wales were in easy reach of a canal.

Source L

It will be shown that it has taken longer to pass goods from Liverpool to Manchester, than to bring them over from America to Liverpool. It will be shown, that often goods have taken twenty-one days in coming from America to Liverpool, and that they have stayed upon the wharfs before they could get the means of conveyance to Manchester for more than six weeks. In summertime, there is often a shortage of water, obliging boats to go half-loaded. In winter they are sometimes locked-up with frost for weeks on end.

(Evidence given to Parliament to support the proposal to build the Manchester to Liverpool Railway. The speaker was criticising canals)

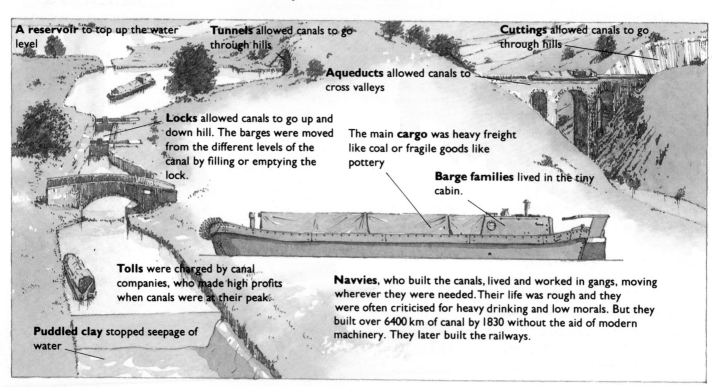

A reservoir to top up the water level

Tunnels allowed canals to go through hills

Cuttings allowed canals to go through hills

Aqueducts allowed canals to cross valleys

Locks allowed canals to go up and down hill. The barges were moved from the different levels of the canal by filling or emptying the lock.

The main cargo was heavy freight like coal or fragile goods like pottery

Barge families lived in the tiny cabin.

Tolls were charged by canal companies, who made high profits when canals were at their peak.

Navvies, who built the canals, lived and worked in gangs, moving wherever they were needed. Their life was rough and they were often criticised for heavy drinking and low morals. But they built over 6400 km of canal by 1830 without the aid of modern machinery. They later built the railways.

Puddled clay stopped seepage of water

How canals worked

CANALS AT WORK – THEIR BENEFITS AND DEFECTS

1 Why were canals so expensive to build?
2 Look at the map. Why were most canals built in the North and Midlands?
3 The list on the opposite page shows the main benefits of canals.
    a How did canals improve the life of ordinary people?
    b Which three benefits do you think were the most important? Explain your answers.
4 What disadvantages of canals are described in Source L?
5 Do you think that canals produced more changes than the improved roads?
6 If canals were soon replaced by railways, does this mean they were of little value?

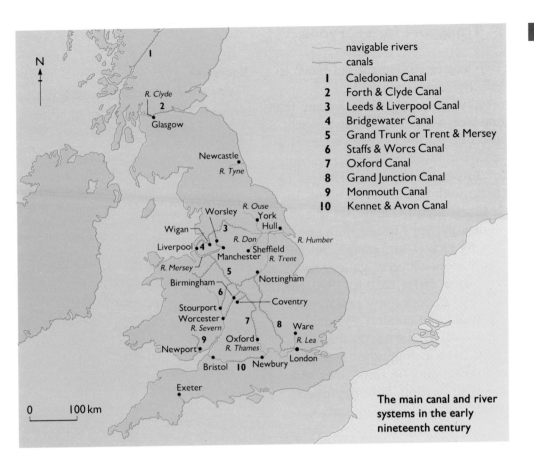

navigable rivers
canals

1	Caledonian Canal
2	Forth & Clyde Canal
3	Leeds & Liverpool Canal
4	Bridgewater Canal
5	Grand Trunk or Trent & Mersey
6	Staffs & Worcs Canal
7	Oxford Canal
8	Grand Junction Canal
9	Monmouth Canal
10	Kennet & Avon Canal

The main canal and river systems in the early nineteenth century

The effects of canals – A better life?

● Some investors made great profits which they invested in other new methods of transport.

● Lower transport costs meant cheap coal, iron, and clay for factories, and cheap building materials for houses.

● New towns grew up as industries were attracted to canals.

● Toll and lock keepers, and bargees gained employment on canals.

● Canal building developed new engineering techniques.

Railways

On 27 September 1825, a steam locomotive called *Locomotion* pulled a train from Stockton to Darlington. On 15 September 1830, the Prime Minister, the Duke of Wellington, opened a railway between Liverpool and Manchester and was carried along the line by a locomotive called *The Rocket* which could reach speeds of 80 k.p.h. The Stockton to Darlington Railway was the first public goods railway and the Liverpool to Manchester line was the first major passenger railway. Both were designed by George and Robert Stephenson.

Many people were not convinced that railways would catch on. Some actually believed that speeds of over 50 k.p.h. were a serious health hazard. Despite this opposition, in 1831 the Liverpool to Manchester line carried over 445,000 people and by 1835 it was making profits of

over £200,000 a year. Not surprisingly, there was a rush to put money into railways and many new lines were built. The early railways were privately owned but, like turnpikes and canals, they needed an Act of Parliament before they could go ahead.

Source M

The Stephenson's showed that reliable locomotives could be constructed. Between 1829 and 1850, locomotive engineering improved further, producing fast, efficient engines for passenger and freight transport. By 1850 railways were carrying more goods than canals.

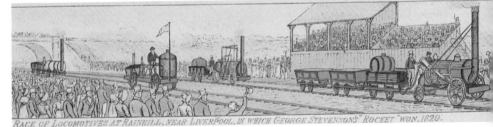

OPENING OF THE FIRST ENGLISH RAIL-WAY BETWEEN STOCKTON AND DARLINGTON. SEPT. 27TH. 1825.

RACE OF LOCOMOTIVES AT RAINHILL, NEAR LIVERPOOL, IN WHICH GEORGE STEVENSONS' ROCKET WON, 1829.

≋ Transport for everyone

Two acts of Parliament did much to help the later development of railways. In 1844, it became law that one train a day had to run in each direction through every station at a charge of no more than 1d per mile (or 2p per 8 kilometres). This led to the growth of third-class travel. In 1848 the Broad Gauge Act forced all new railways to use the same 4 foot 8½ inch (1.4 m) gauge. Before this, various different gauges had been used. From 1850 to 1900, the railway network grew rapidly and the speed and comfort of travel improved. By the 1890s, mainline trains were averaging over 95 k.p.h. and passengers on some lines had access to heating, lighting, toilets, dining cars and sleeping cars.

Source N

Railroads have one disadvantage in the carriage of coal for factories. The banks of the canals are generally studded with factories. Coals, carried in boats, are lodged without any extra expense at their doors. The railroads are otherwise circumstanced. The coal is deposited by them at 'stations' from where it must be carried to its destination.

(James Wheeler, 1835)

Source O

It was declared that the railway would prevent cows grazing and hens laying. The poisoned air from the locomotive would kill birds as they flew over them. Houses next to the line would be burnt up from the fire thrown from the engine chimneys. The air would be polluted by clouds of smoke. There would no longer be any use for horses, and there would be no use for oats and hay.

(Samuel Smiles, commenting in 1857 on the different ideas people had about the effects of railways)

Source P

What can be more palpably absurd than the prospect held out of locomotives travelling twice as fast as stage-coaches?

(*The Quarterly Review*, 1825. The smoke and sparks upset people and they also truly believed that the human body could not stand up to the speed of rail travel)

George Stephenson

Isambard Kingdom Brunel
1806–59

Brunel was an engineer of genius. He was appointed Chief Engineer to the Great Western Railway at the age of 25 and built many of the lines in the region. These lines avoided sharp curves and steep gradients and used a 7 foot (2.1 m) broad gauge which allowed the trains to travel at higher speeds with greater comfort.
Unfortunately, most other lines used a narrower gauge, and in 1846 Parliament refused to allow Brunel's system to be used outside the Great Western Region.

As well as railways, Brunel designed harbours and bridges such as the Clifton Suspension Bridge. However, his construction of the world's biggest steamship, the *Great Eastern*, failed commercially. His design for an atmospheric railway, using air suction, which would allow trains to travel at 110 k.p.h. without smoke and dirt, was equally unsuccessful.

Source Q
The growth of the rail network, 1845–51

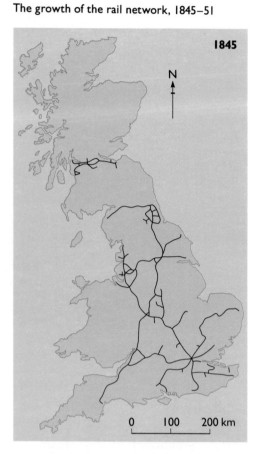

1845

0   100   200 km

1851

0   100   200 km

The effects of railways

New towns grew at rail junctions such as Swindon and Crewe.

Roads and canals declined in importance.

Firms could specialise in a single product and sell it all over the country.

Commuter suburbs grew as people began to travel to work from more pleasant areas.

Quick, cheap transport helped all industries to grow. It provided cheap raw materials and allowed them to sell goods further afield.

Food shortages became rare and diets improved. Perishable foods like fruit, vegetables and fresh fish became readily available.

A FIRST-CLASS TRAIN ON THE LIVERPOOL AND MANCHESTER RAIL-WAY, 1833.

A SECOND-CLASS TRAIN ON THE LIVERPOOL AND MANCHESTER RAIL-WAY, 1833.

Demand for coal, iron and other materials grew to equip the new railways.

Department stores grew up as things could be produced in one place and moved all over the country.

National sports developed. A football league and similar competitions became possible.

People could go on holiday or on day trips. Resorts like Blackpool grew.

A national standard time was introduced as trains had to keep to an accurate schedule. Before this the time in different areas varied.

National newspapers developed and could be delivered every day. People began to take more interest in news and politics.

CHANGES: RAILWAYS AND THEIR EFFECTS

1 Why would turnpike and canal owners oppose railways?

2 What other arguments were put forward against railways?

3 Study Sources M, O, P, and Q. Explain why you think the opponents of railways began to give up their arguments.

4 How did rail travel change between 1831 and 1900?

5 Did railways make life better or worse? Explain your answer.

6 Which effects of railways would you say were the most important and which were the least important? Explain your answer.

New forms of transport and communication

Major developments in transport and communication

1837	Telegraph invented
1840	'Penny post' introduced by Rowland Hill
1850	Telegraph cable laid across the English Channel
1866	Telegraph cable laid across the Atlantic
1876	Telephone invented by Alexander Graham Bell
1884	Daimler drove a motorcycle with a petrol engine
1885	Benz drove a car with a petrol engine
1885	Safety bicycle invented
1885	Trams were first electrified
1888	Pneumatic tyre invented by John Dunlop
1894	The steam-turbine first used to power ships. This allowed much greater speeds
1896	*Daily Mail* launched
1896	Red Flag Act repealed

At first, the Railway Age led to a decline in the use of roads. But by 1900, new types of private and public road transport were emerging. Bicycles grew in popularity; the penny-farthing, with its massive front wheel and small back wheel, had been used in the 1870s, but the major breakthroughs occurred when the modern style of safety bicycle and the pneumatic tyre were invented. Petrol engines were invented by the Germans, Gottfried Daimler and Carl Benz, but the motor car was slow to develop in Britain owing to the Red Flag Act. This said that motorised vehicles could not travel at more than 4 m.p.h. (6.5 k.p.h.) and that a man carrying a red flag had to walk in front of them. When the Act was repealed in 1896 motor cars became more popular.

Major developments in public road transport occurred in cities.

Horse-drawn buses had been in use throughout the nineteenth century and trams were used after 1880. The electric tram, introduced in 1885, was cheaper, quicker and more efficient. It allowed people to travel across the city more rapidly for work or leisure. Travel overseas also became easier and quicker after 1850, with the use of steel steamships and great ocean-going liners. By 1900, serious attempts to build flying machines were well underway.

Other forms of communication also developed rapidly after 1840. Rowland Hill introduced the 'penny post'. This used adhesive stamps and replaced the old system where letters were charged by weight and paid for by the person who received them. The telegraph allowed instant communication. This was a way of sending messages along wires, using electricity. By 1850, it took the form of an alphabet of dots and dashes called Morse Code and was in wide use. Soon Britain was linked by telegraph to places as far away as the USA and India.

The telephone was invented in 1876 and was in wide use by the 1880s. By 1900 the first steps had also been made in wireless communication by Marconi. The telegraph and telephone meant that news could be rapidly gathered from all parts of the world. These further encouraged the growth of national newspapers, like the *Daily Mail*, designed to appeal to ordinary people.

Source R

An early car led by a man with a red flag

NEW FORMS OF COMMUNICATION

1 What changes in communications took place after 1840?
2 Changes in communications were happening very quickly. Why do you think this was?
3 Do you think these changes made people's lives better or worse?
4 Think back across all the changes in transport and communications in this chapter. Did they make people's lives better or worse?

Living conditions in towns

What makes people well off? It is not only how much money they have. It is also the quality of their diet, the type of clothes they wear, the state of their health and houses, and how safe they feel. The way the elderly or unemployed are treated is also important to many people.

Between 1750 and 1900 the great changes in agriculture, industry and communications changed where and how people lived. Towns grew rapidly near the new factories or at places where different transport routes met. The people who moved to the new towns usually went there in search of work. Some had been forced to move out of the nearby countryside due to enclosures. Others came from poorer areas further away, like Ireland. All of them hoped to improve their living conditions and there is no doubt that the wages of ordinary people rose throughout the nineteenth century. investigate whether or not these higher wages actually made the lives of ordinary people in towns better. To do this you will look at food, clothes and household goods, housing, health, crime and the treatment of those without work.

INVESTIGATION

1 Draw the chart below. As you conduct your investigation you should complete it. Use the map and list below to answer the following questions:
2 Where were the towns with the most rapid growth located?
3 What do you think were the most important reasons for town growth?

Town Growth, 1801–31
The increase of population in England and Wales in thirty years, 1801 to 1831, has been more than 47%. The number of inhabitants of five of our most important towns has grown by more than double that rate; being Manchester 109%, Glasgow 108%, Birmingham 73%, Leeds 99%, Liverpool 100%, giving an average of almost 98%.

(Report of the Select Committee on the Health of Towns, 1840)

Major causes of town growth

● Rising Population
● Agricultural changes. New methods of farming and new machines meant fewer jobs in the countryside
● Poverty and unemployment in Ireland
● New jobs available in factories

Changing living conditions, 1750–1900

	Better	The same	Worse
Food/clothes/ household goods			
Housing			
Health			
Crime/law and order			
The jobless			

🔁 Food, clothes and household goods

Source A

The weekly income and expenditure of a typical family of textile workers in the early nineteenth century.

Income	
1st boy aged 15 *feeder*	30p
2nd boy aged 14 *piecer*	20p
3rd boy aged 13 *piecer*	10p
4th girl aged 10 *carder*	2p
5th girl aged 7	
6th girl aged 3	
Self, Wife *Spinner*	90p
Total weekly income	**£1.52**

Items purchased		
Flour	Candles	Coal
Meal	Meat	Tea or coffee
Yeast	Cheese	Worsted
Soap	Sugar	Rent
Butter	Potatoes	
Total weekly expenditure		**£1.42**
Balance left over		10p

Ordinary people who moved to the towns probably hoped for work with higher wages. This would mean they could afford better and more varied food and clothing and even a few luxuries. Certainly many were better off but, although the price of clothes fell between 1750 and 1900, many families still found it hard to afford new clothing or a new pair of shoes. In fact, according to Charles Booth and Seebohm Rowntree, who carried out surveys of living conditions in the late nineteenth century, over 30 per cent of the people still lived in poverty, unable to afford adequate clothing and food.

If they fell ill there was no National Health Service to help them. If they lost their jobs there was no unemployment benefit. Nor was there an old age pension to look forward to when they grew old. Drink and gambling were often their only escapes.

Source B

Inside a poor labourers cottage in Dorset

Source C

The income and expenditure of an agricultural labourer's family, consisting of a couple with five young children, in the early nineteenth century

Expenditure		
Flour	33 litres	32p
Yeast	(to make it into bread)	1p
Salt		1p
Bacon	450 g boiled with greens; the pot-liquor with bread and potatoes makes a mess for the children	3p
Tea	30 g	1p
Sugar	100 g	2p
Butter	200 g (or lard)	1p
Soap	100 g	1p
Candles	150 g	1p
Thread	for mending apparel	1p
Total weekly expenditure		**44p**

Income	
The man receives the common weekly wages 8 months in the year of	35p
By task work in the remaining 4 months, he earns something more. His extra earnings, if equally divided among the 52 weeks in the year, would increase the weekly wages by	5p
The wife's common work is to bake bread for the family, to wash and mend ragged clothes, and to look after the family, but at the beansetting, haymaking and harvest, she earns an average weekly wage throughout the year of	2p
Total weekly income	**42p**
Weekly expenses of this family	44p
Weekly income	42p
Deficiency of income	2p

DAILY LIFE

1. What are the main items of household expenditure?
2. What essentials are missing from the lists of expenditure?
3. Are any of the items on the lists luxuries?
4. Use Source D to help you make a similar weekly menu for the families in A and C.

Menu of meals provided during week ending 23 June 1900

	Breakfast	Dinner	Tea	Supper
Friday	Bread, butter, and tea	Bacon, potatoes, and rhubarb pie	Bread, butter, lettuce, and tea	Bread, brawn, and coffee
Saturday	Fried bacon, bread, tea	Fish and potatoes	Bread, butter, and tea	Bread and cheese
Sunday	Fried bacon, bread, tea	Stewed rabbit, potatoes, cabbage, Yorkshire pudding	Bread, butter, sweet cake, lettuce, tea	Bread and cheese
Monday	Fried bacon, bread, tea	Rabbit, potatoes, rhubarb pie	Bread, butter, sweet cake, tea	Rhubarb pie
Tuesday	Fried bacon, bread, tea	Roast pork, potatoes, Yorkshire pudding	Bread, butter, tea	Rhubarb pie
Wednesday	Fried bacon, bread, tea	Cold pork, potatoes	Bread, butter, tea	Bread, cheese, and coffee
Thursday	Bread, butter, tea	Cold pork, potatoes, suet pudding	Bread, butter, sweet cake, tea	Brawn, bread, and coffee

Statement of income and expenditure for eight weeks

Wages: eight weeks at £1	£8.00
Food	£4.35
Rent and rates	£1.26
Coal at £1.20 ton	£0.68
Gas (0.42p in slot meter)	£0.10
Soap	£0.10
Sundries	£0.08
Sick Club	£0.20
Life Insurance	£0.07
Clothing Club	£0.10
Kept by husband	£0.80
Surplus	**£0.26**

Source D

The income, expenditure and diet of a labouring family in 1900

This family consists of five persons, a father, aged 49, mother, 47, and three daughters, age respectively 22, 13, 8. The mother 'has a bad leg' and the eldest daughter is not strong enough to go out to work, as she is 'suffering from weakness,' which takes the form of rheumatism. The two younger children are at school.

There is a deficiency of 40 per cent in the protein of this family's diet, and a deficiency of 41 per cent in its fuel value.

(From *Poverty: A Study in Town Life* by Seebohm Rowntree, 1901)

Source E
Rich household in 1867

5 Does Rowntree's comment about the food and fuel deficiencies in D hold good for A and C?

6 Why would the family in D join a sick club and pay life insurance?

7 List the differences in clothing, furniture and household goods between the families in Sources B and E.

8 Fill in your chart (see page 39).

Housing and health

Problems

The rich and middle classes of the towns lived in large villas with servants and large gardens. Life was very different for many ordinary people. The sources explain the major housing problems in many new towns and show how they led to health problems.

Source F

The chief sewerage is open channels and the whole soil is saturated with sewerage water. The sewers discharge into the brook or basin of the canal. The water of this basin is so charged with decaying matter that in hot weather bubbles of sulphurated hydrogen are continually rising to the surface. The stench is very strong, fevers prevail all around.

(Report on the sanitary condition of Bradford, James Smith, 1845)

Source G

Poor housing conditions in Church Lane, Bloomsbury, London in 1875

Source H

The streets of Leeds are very much as in all old towns. Fortunately for Leeds the main street is of ample width and there are many cheerful, open streets where the better classes reside. The lower classes, here as elsewhere, inhabit the less healthy localities.

By far the most unhealthy localities of Leeds are close squares of houses, or yards, as they are called, which have been erected for the accommodation of working people. Some of these are airless from the enclosed structure, and unprovided with any form of under-drainage, or convenience, or arrangements for cleansing, are one mass of damp and filth. The ashes, garbage, and filth of all kinds are thrown from the doors and windows of the houses upon the surface of the streets. The privies are few in proportion to the number of inhabitants. They are open to view both in front and rear, in a filthy condition and often remain without the removal of any filth for six months. A vast amount of ill-health prevails, inducing a desire for spirits and opiates, increasing poverty and premature deaths.

(Report by James Smith, a commissioner appointed to investigate the sanitary conditions in towns, 1845)

Source I

The poorer districts of Liverpool often have rough ground in which there are pits. In autumn there is a good deal of water in them, in which there have been thrown dead dogs and cats and other offensive things. This water is used for cooking. I could not believe this. I thought it was only used for washing. Was that because there was no other water supply? There is a good supply of water for the poor, if they had something to keep it in. The water is turned on for four hours a day. Each poor person fetches as much as they can in pans, but they have few of these and soon run out of water.

(J. Riddall Wood, evidence to Parliament, 1840)

EVIDENCE: LIVING IN TOWNS

1 List the defects in nineteenth-century towns. Use the following headings: Housing quality; Quality of water supply; Sewage disposal; Quality of air; Disease.
2 Are the written sources or illustrations more useful for an investigation of nineteenth-century town life?
3 Do you think Source H provides reliable evidence about conditions in nineteenth-century towns?
4 What can a historian learn from Source G?
5 Why were there so many outbreaks of diseases like cholera and typhus in nineteenth-century towns?
6 Why would the rich as well as the poor worry about these diseases?

Solutions

Many attempts were made to solve the problems of poor housing and disease. By 1900, sewers, drains, public toilets and large parks could be found in most major cities. New houses were being built and people could use a wide range of shops. Important medical changes also helped improve people's lives. In 1871 the average age at which people died was still only 45. By 1911 the average life expectancy for men was 50, and for women, it was 55.

Source J

Good housing on the Shaftesbury Park Estate in London, 1874.

Despite the growth of good quality housing in many cities, as late as 1900 Charles Booth found many people living in conditions like those described in Source H.

Source K

There was a great development in the skill of doctors. In 1796 Edward Jenner discovered vaccination as a means of preventing small-pox. In 1847 James Simpson first used chloroform to kill pain during an operation. This opened the way to surgical achievements hitherto impossible.

However, the growth in the number of operations gravely increased the risks of infection in hospital. Joseph Lister cleaned the hands of the surgeon and his instruments and kept the air sprayed with powerful antiseptic throughout operations. These methods prevented infection. Anaesthetics had made operations painless; antiseptics made them safer.

(C. P. Hill, a historian writing in 1957. Other late nineteenth-century developments included better standards of nursing, the use of X-rays, and Louis Pasteur's discovery that germs caused diseases. After this innoculations began which stopped the threat of the great killer diseases like cholera and typhoid)

Source L
Government action
1848 Public Health Act
● Board of Health was set up to improve public health.
● The Board could set up Local Boards of Health in areas with high death rates to make sure no new houses were built without drains or toilets.
● If water companies could provide water for 1p a week, the Local Board could force people to have piped water in their houses.
● The Local Board could charge a rate to pay for improvements.
1875 Public Health Act
● Local Government should lay sewers and drains, and build reservoirs, swimming baths, parks and public toilets.
● Local health inspectors appointed.
1875 Artisans' Dwellings Act
● Local Councils were given the power to clear slums.
● New houses had to have walls of a good thickness, piped water, toilets and damp proofing.

IMPROVEMENTS

1 Which of the problems you listed in question 1 on page 42 might be solved by these ideas?
2 How successful do you think each solution would be?
3 Why would some middle-class people object to the solutions?
4 How is Source J an improvement on earlier nineteenth-century housing?

5 Why were parks and a range of shops important?
6 Why do you think problems like those in Source H still existed in 1900 despite the new Health and Housing laws of 1848 and 1875?
7 Fill in your chart (see page 39).

Elizabeth Fry 1780–1845

Elizabeth Fry (seated left with book) was a Quaker from a wealthy family. In 1813 she was asked to visit the women in Newgate Prison. She was disgusted by the conditions and began to campaign for reform. She called for changes in the way women and children were kept. She tried to teach the prisoners' children and to spread the Christian message. Her ideas influenced the prison reforms of Robert Peel.

Source M

In visiting prisons I was sorry to see children so exposed to the wickedness of certain women. The first words the children spoke were swear words. Women who came to prison weeping over their crimes would be laughing and joking by the time of their trial. They seem to have been trained for almost any crime whilst in prison. It therefore struck me that it was important to separate women and children from the hardened criminals.

(Elizabeth Fry, writing in the early nineteenth century)

Prisoners in the exercise yard at Newgate Prison, 1872

⊃ Crime, law and order

People who could not find work in towns often turned to crime. Crime was a major problem partly because the watchmen employed to keep order were often old or incompetent. Even the special constables in London could not always cope. Partly because of this the laws were very severe. Before 1823 over 200 crimes were punishable by death. These included thefts of over 5p and writing your name on Westminster Bridge!

Many other crimes were punished by transportation – banishment – to the colonies, or by a public whipping or prison. In prisons the guilty and those waiting for trial were all put together. Rich prisoners could pay to live in luxury but the poor had to pay 0.5p a day for the little food they got. Those found not guilty could not leave prison until they paid their gaol fees.

Source N

A boy, only twelve years of age, was committed to the borough gaol. His father was dead, his mother lived in a cellar in one of the lowest streets of the town. She could just support herself, and left the boy to pick up a living as best he could. I said to him, 'If I could obtain some sort of situation for you where you could earn an honest living would you try to do better?' He burst into tears as he assured me I would never have cause to repent it. My hope was to have got him into an institution for destitute children but I was unable to obtain it, and the boy was discharged. Two days after I opened the door of a cell and to my surprise found him again an inmate. Looking at me with an almost hopeless expression of anguish he said, 'Sir, what could I do?' and then told me his tale. On leaving gaol he went to look for his mother. She was gone into the workhouse. Penniless and houseless he wandered about all day and night in the streets. The next day, driven by hunger, he stole some bread and was committed for the offence. He said anything was better than his condition outside. Shortly after, an officer looked into his cell and found the unhappy boy suspended by a hammock girth to the gas-pipe, dead.

(Report by the Chaplain of Manchester Gaol, 1853)

Attempted solutions

Many different methods were tried to reduce crime and there is no doubt that crime declined in most cities after 1850.

Source O
1823 Prisons Act
- Gaolers could no longer make money selling food and privileges.
- Women prisoners were to have women warders.
- Prisoners were to have lessons in reading, writing and religion.

Source P
1820 Whipping for women offenders was abolished.

1822–37 The death penalty was phased out for all crimes except murder and treason.

1835 Prison Inspectors were introduced and a prison building programme was stepped up. Gradually, prisons were made much stricter and children were separated from older prisoners. All prisoners had to work, many had to do hard labour.

1853 Transportation of criminals to Australia was ended.

1878 All prisons were placed under government control.

Source Q
Streetlighting
The introduction of gas street lighting and then electric lighting helped improve people's safety.

CAUSES AND CONSEQUENCES: LAW AND ORDER

1. Why was there a lot of crime in towns?
2. Before 1837 juries often refused to convict criminals even if they were guilty. Can you explain why?
3. Why would each of the solutions shown in sources O–R reduce crime?
4. Which solution do you think was the most important?
5. Living standards rose after 1850. Do you think this helped reduce crime? Explain your answer.
6. Fill in your chart (see page 39)

Sir Robert Peel 1788–1850

Peel became Home Secretary in 1822. He realised that there were not enough trained police to control crime in London. Often soldiers had to be called in to keep order. So he set up the Metropolitan Police. Peel also introduced a series of prison reforms. He later went on to become the Prime Minister who abolished the Corn Laws.

Source R

A new police force in the City of Westminster shall be in charge of one Metropolitan Police District. A number of fit and able men shall act as constables for preserving the peace and preventing robberies and other felonies and catching criminals.

(Metropolitan Police Act, 1829)

Source S

Metropolitan Police, 1851.
The idea of a police force was successful and spread to other towns after 1829. By 1856 every County and Borough was forced by law to maintain a police force.

Source T

Inmates of a workhouse, 1843. On entering workhouses families would often be split up and forced to live separate lives. Women, men and the elder children all had separate dormitories and work areas.

Edwin Chadwick 1800–90

Chadwick was the most influential author of the report on the poor law that led to the 1834 Poor Law Amendment Act. He hated waste and severely attacked the old systems of poor relief under which parishes often just paid an allowance to the unemployed poor. Chadwick felt this was a mistake and just encouraged idleness. Instead he put forward the solution outlined in Source U. He was also responsible for many important public health reforms in the nineteenth century.

The very poor

There were many poor people in the new towns who simply could not make a living. Today, the social services usually try to help people in need. For many in the nineteenth century there was only the workhouse. Workhouses were made much harsher by the 1834 Poor Law Amendment Act. The threat of entry into a workhouse was a constant nightmare for those without work or those who were old and had no relatives to look after them. The new law was so unpopular that there were violent attacks on workhouses in many areas. In fact, the New Poor Law did not work in the North but, with some alterations which made it a little less harsh, it continued beyond 1900 in the South.

Source U

To encourage industry and thrift, it will be necessary to make the state of being a pauper less attractive than that of the worse paid labourer. Secondly, we need to make sure that only those in genuine need receive poor relief. One way of doing this would be to hand out relief only to those willing to enter a workhouse.

(Edwin Chadwick, Report of the Royal Commission on the Poor Law, 1832–34. These ideas formed the basis of the 1834 Poor Law Amendment Act)

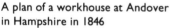

A plan of a workhouse at Andover in Hampshire in 1846

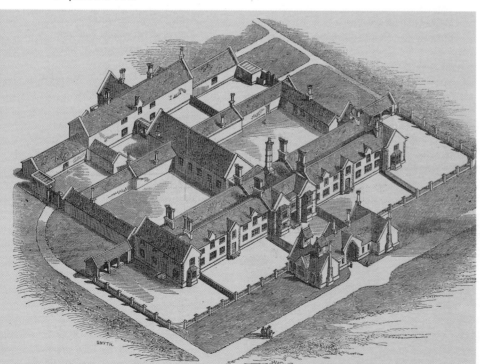

Source V

Workhouse Routine

All the paupers in the work-house, except the sick and in-sane, and the paupers of the first, fourth and seventh classes, shall rise, be set to work, leave off work, and go to bed at the times mentioned in the Form.

	Time of rising	Interval for breakfast	Time for work	Interval for dinner	Time for work	Interval for supper	Time for going to bed
From 25 March to 29 Sept	5.45 am	6.30 - 7	7 - 12	12 - 1	1 - 6	6 - 7	8 pm
From 29 Sept to 25 March	6.45 am	7.30 - 8	8 - 12	12 - 1	1 - 6	6 - 7	8 pm

(From rules drawn up by the poor law commissioners in their Annual Reports between 1835 and 1841)

Source W

Workhouse (Rules of Conduct)

Any pauper who shall make any noise when silence is ordered to be kept;
● Or shall use obscene or profane language;
● Or shall refuse or neglect to work, after having been required to do so;
● Or shall play at cards or other games of chance;

Shall be deemed *disorderly*.

Any pauper who shall within seven days, repeat any one or commit more than one of the offences specified;
● Or shall by word or deed insult the master or matron, or any other officer of the work-house, or any of the Guardians;
● Or shall be drunk;
● Or shall wilfully disturb the other inmates during prayers or divine worship;
Shall be deemed *refractory*.

It shall be lawful for the master of the workhouse to punish any *disorderly* pauper by substituting, during a period of not greater than forty-eight hours, for his or her dinner, as prescribed by the dietary, a meal consisting of eight ounces [225 g] of bread or one pound [450 g] of cooked potatoes and also by withholding from him during the same period, all butter, cheese, sugar, or broth.

And it shall be lawful for the Board of Guardians to order any *refractory* pauper to be punished by confinement to a separate room, with or without alteration to the diet for up to twenty-four hours.

(Rules drawn up by the Poor Law Commissioners in their seventh Annual Report, 1841)

Source X

This diet sheet for inmates was produced by the Easterly Union of Workhouses in East Kent in 1835

Breakfast and supper	
men	170g of bread with 30g of cheese or 15g of butter
women	140g of bread with 30g of cheese or 15g of butter
Dinner	
Day 1 men	450g of meat pudding + vegetables
women	280g of meat pudding + vegetables
Day 2 men	200g of bread with 30g of cheese
women	200g of bread with 30g of cheese
Day 3 men	450g of suet pudding + vegetables
women	280g of suet pudding + vegetables
Day 4 men	200g of bread with 30g of cheese
women	200g of bread with 30g of cheese
Day 5 men	450g of suet pudding + vegetables
women	280g of suet pudding + vegetables
Day 6 men	200g of bread with 30g of cheese
women	200g of bread with 30g of cheese
Day 7 men	200g of bread with 30g of cheese
women	200g of bread with 30g of cheese

PEOPLE IN THE PAST: POOR LAW

1 In Source U what does Chadwick say is the reason for harsh workhouses?
2 What do Sources T to X tell you about life in the workhouse? Look at living conditions, diet and work.
3 What does the workhouse suggest about Victorian people's attitudes to poverty?

4 Fill in your chart.
● Living conditions improved between 1750 and 1900 for all people.
● Living conditions got worse between 1750 and 1900 for all people.
● Living conditions improved between 1750 and 1900 for many people.

Workhouse routine

The work given to people in the workhouse was hard and monotonous. Typical jobs included breaking bones or unravelling ropes and removing the tar from them which was known as picking oakum. All workhouse inmates had to wear uniform.

Investigating political changes, 1750–1900

Riots were common in the late eighteenth and early nineteenth centuries. Ordinary people had few other ways of complaining or showing how they felt about things. These are the Gordon Riots in 1780.

This chapter is about the political changes that took place in Britain between 1750 and 1900. You will be investigating whether ordinary people had more say in how the country was governed. For example, could more people take part in elections? Did these changes improve people's lives?

In Britain today, we are used to the idea of democracy – where members of a community or organisation have a say in making important decisions. For example, almost everybody over the age of 18 can vote to elect a Member of Parliament (MP). Voters can choose from a number of candidates, who represent different political parties, each with different policies.

There are many other ways in which we can help to influence political decisions and make sure our opinions are heard. We can vote in local elections, join pressure groups, or write to newspapers.

At work, too, people can have a say in what goes on by joining trade unions, which negotiate with employers over working conditions, hours of work and pay. Unions can also help to protect their members. In some cases, trade unions will even call their members out on strike.

There are also many laws which help to protect people and their property, and which are meant to make sure that nobody is discriminated against because of their gender, ethnic group or religion. These laws affect every part of our daily lives – at home, at school and at work.

We often take all these rights for granted. However, almost none of them existed in 1750. How many of them do you think had been achieved by 1900? Copy the chart on the left. It contains a number of statements. Put a tick if you think the statement accurately describes the situation in the years mentioned. The first one has been done for you. As you work through this chapter check to see whether your first answers were correct.

	1750	1900	Today
The King or Queen has to give his or her approval before Acts of Parliament become law.	✓	✓	✓
Nearly all adults over the age of 18 have the right to vote.			
Nearly all adults over the age of 18 have the right to stand for election as an MP.			
Voting is done secretly, using a ballot box.			
Most working adults have the right to join a trade union.			
Men and women are meant to receive the same levels of pay for doing similar jobs.			

▥ The changing role of the monarchy

People today have mixed views about the monarchy. Some regard the Royal Family as a luxury which the country no longer needs. Others see the Royal Family as still having a valuable part in British life. All would agree, however, that nowadays the monarch has almost no political power.

In the late eighteenth century, the monarch was very powerful. George II (1727–1760) and George III (1760–1820) both played an active part in politics. However, as the amount of government business increased, especially after the French Wars (1793–1815), Parliament, and particularly the House of Commons, became more important. Many people believed it was wrong for an unelected King or Queen to interfere with government policies.

By 1830, the Prime Minister had more political power than the monarch, and took the leading role in appointing government ministers and deciding on policies. Queen Victoria accepted this, and although she was usually consulted by her Prime Ministers, during her reign (1837–1901) the monarchy became more of a figurehead. Victoria was not always popular, but people still looked up to the Royal Family, and followed its example.

Queen Victoria (1837–1901)

Although the monarchy became less powerful while she was Queen, she became personally more popular. Her long reign was enthusiastically celebrated in her Diamond Jubilee in 1897.

George III (1760–1820)

Grandson of George II. He was anxious to influence government policy, but often made unpopular and unwise decisions. Usually blamed as the king who 'lost' the American colonies. He lost his influence after he became afflicted by porphyria, a form of madness, and, after 1811, his son ruled as Regent.

The power of the crown in 1760 and 1900	
George III – 1760	**Victoria – 1900**
Head of State. Head of the Church of England.	Head of State. Head of Church of England.
Decided on government policy – especially foreign affairs.	Little influence on government policy.
Had to give his approval ('the Royal Assent') before an Act of Parliament became law.	Had to give 'the Royal Assent' before an Act of Parliament became law.
Chose Prime Minister and other government ministers.	No role in choosing Prime Minister and other government ministers.
Controlled election of about 30 MPs, and chose senior army and navy officers.	No role in controlling election of MPs or appointing senior army and navy officers.

The reform of Parliament

These pages look at Parliament in the late eighteenth and early nineteenth centuries. Study the evidence carefully. Do you think Parliament was able to represent the interests of all British people fairly and equally?

Political parties

Until the early nineteenth century, there were no political parties with different ideas or policies. Some MPs regarded themselves as 'Whigs', some as 'Tories', but there was usually little to choose between them. Most MPs felt that Parliament's job was to make sure the country could defend itself from foreign enemies and disturbances at home. At elections, voters chose between individual candidates rather than different policies.

Who could become an MP?

Only men who owned land and property above a certain value could stand as MPs. MPs were unpaid, so only a wealthy man could afford to become one. Naturally, they usually made sure that laws would not be passed which might threaten their interests.

Constituencies

There were two main types. Each county returned two MPs. There were also 'borough' seats, each of which had two MPs. In the Middle Ages, boroughs had usually been quite important towns, but many had declined in importance by the late eighteenth century.

Major towns without MPs in 1800:

Leeds, Manchester, Birmingham, Bradford

Boroughs with MPs:

Old Sarum (a hill in Wiltshire)
Dunwich (most of which had sunk beneath the North Sea)
Bossiney (a Cornish borough with one voter)

Source B

The county of Yorkshire, which contains near a million of souls, sends two county members; and so does the county of Rutland, which contains not a hundredth part of that number. The town of Old Sarum, which contains not three houses, sends two members; and the town of Manchester, which contains upwards of sixty thousand souls, is not admitted to send any. Is there any principle in these things?

(Thomas Paine, *Rights of Man*, 1791)

Who could vote?

Only men could vote – and very few of them. In 1831 only 5 per cent of the population were allowed to vote. Scotland, with a population of over two million, had an electorate of under 4000. In county seats, only men who owned land above a certain value ('forty shilling freeholders') could vote. This sum had been fixed in 1430, and the decline in money values by the eighteenth century meant that the number of voters had increased. Voting rights varied in boroughs. In some, like Bury St Edmunds, only members of the town council voted. In 'scot and lot' boroughs, like Northampton, all male householders who paid local rates could vote.

Source A

An Election in 1817. There was no secret ballot. Voting was held openly. Electors could be bribed or bullied into voting for a particular candidate. Very often only one candidate stood for election. In seats where there was a choice of candidate, huge sums of money were spent in persuading voters. One candidate spent £100,000 in the 1807 election, trying to win a county seat in Yorkshire. He lost.

'Patronage'

Many MPs, particularly for 'rotten' boroughs, like Old Sarum, were controlled by local landowners. These landowners could instruct tenants and local residents to vote for the candidate they chose. About 270 MPs were controlled in this way. They supported the interests of their 'patrons' in debates and votes in the House of Commons, trying to prevent any changes which would weaken their wealth and influence.

One MP described his feelings after being elected at Appleby.

Source C

The Fact is that yesterday morning between 11 and 12, I was unanimously elected by one Elector, to represent this borough in Parliament. There was no other Candidate, no opposition, no Poll demanded, scrutiny or petition. So I had nothing to do but thank the said Elector for the Unanimous Voice by which I was chosen. On Friday Morning I shall quit this Triumphant scene with flying colours, and a noble Determination not to see it again in less than seven years.

(Sir Philip Francis, 1802)

Source D

That honourable House of Commons, in its present state, is evidently far too removed in habits, wealth and station, from the wants and interests of the lower and middle classes of the people. The great aristocratical interests of all kinds are well represented there, but the interests of Industry and of Trade have scarcely any representatives at all!

(Declaration of the Birmingham Political Union, 1830)

Total No of MPs	
England	489
Wales	24
Scotland	45
Ireland (after 1801)	100

The House of Commons in 1793. Can you see any similarities with the House of Commons today? Are there any differences?

EVIDENCE: THE NEED FOR PARLIAMENTARY REFORM

1 Study Sources A, B and C. What does each source tell you about the need for changes?

2 How useful is Source A for finding out about what happened during an election at this time? Explain your answer.

3 Which Source do you think best illustrates the unfairness of elections at this time? Explain your choice.

4 Source B was written by Thomas Paine, who was a strong critic of the way politics was organised at the time. Does this mean his evidence should not be used by historians?

5 Source C was written by an MP, Sir Philip Francis. He appears to be quite happy with the way politics was organised at the time. Does this mean his evidence should not be used by historians?

6 Study Source D. From what you have read so far, would you agree with the points made in this Declaration?

7 Do you think there was a need for changes in political life? Explain your answer, making sure you mention the following points:
- who could become an MP;
- size of constituencies;
- who could vote;
- how voting took place;
- patronage.

8 If you have just argued that there was a clear need for change at this time, can you suggest why the parliamentary system had lasted for so long?

Now check your chart. Do you need to change anything?

The 1832 Reform Act

Imagine that the tree stands for the country as a whole. Political figures usually belong to one of the following types. Conservatives want to keep the tree (the country) more or less as it has always been. Reformers want to make important changes – by chopping down some branches (e.g., changing laws). Radicals want to uproot the tree completely (e.g., changing politics and society completely).

The 1832 Reform Act was the first attempt to improve the way in which Parliament was elected. These pages examine how and why this reform took place, and how much the Reform Act changed political life.

After 1750, a growing number of people wanted to see reforms in political life. Their main aim was to reduce the power of the King, and that of the wealthy landowners who dominated Parliament. They thought that the best way of doing this was to give the vote to many more people. Then MPs would have to do what the new voters wanted, not what the landowners wanted. These ideas were particularly popular with the growing middle class — merchants and manufacturers, who did not have the vote and resented the political power of the aristocracy.

In August 1819, 80,000 men, women and children met in St. Peter's Fields, Manchester. They came to hear speeches calling for political reform, particularly the right for all men to vote. Magistrates ordered troops to arrest the leading speaker, the radical Henry 'Orator' Hunt. In the panic, eleven people were killed and hundreds more injured. The government congratulated the magistrates for sending in the troops and passed laws making it even more difficult to campaign for political reform. The massacre became known as 'Peterloo', an ironic reference to the Battle of Waterloo. What impression is the cartoonist trying to give of the events at 'Peterloo'?

The reformers were strongly influenced by events in America and France. Revolutions had given ordinary citizens many more rights than existed in Britain. Many working-class people followed events in newspapers and journals and became attracted to the idea of greater equality and political power. After the end of the French Wars in 1815, mass meetings were held at which speakers called for reform, and which began to alarm the government, leading to the events of 'Peterloo' in 1819.

By 1830, the situation was changing, and parliamentary reform seemed more likely. There were several reasons for this:

- Increasing numbers of middle- and working-class people were calling for reform.
- In 1830, a Whig government, led by Lord Grey, came to power. The Whigs were more in favour of reform than the previous Tory government; they hoped to win the support of new middle-class voters. They did not intend to give the vote to many more people, however.
- There was a growing fear in Parliament that people might try to overthrow the government by force unless moderate reforms were introduced.

After a long struggle, during which Tory MPs and the House of Lords tried to block any changes, the Parliamentary Reform Act was passed in June 1832.

Source E

Every sensible man sees the Reform Bill is the commencement of a mighty revolution.

(William Cobbett, a radical journalist)

Source F

The Victory of the People is now secured and seated beyond the fear of accident. By this Act, a mighty and ancient system of corruption will receive its death-blow.

(*The Leeds Mercury*, a newspaper)

The 1832 Reform Act

What changes were made?	What had not changed?
● Many 'rotten' boroughs lost MPs. New boroughs were created, giving growing industrial towns like Manchester, Leeds, Sheffield and Birmingham their own MPs. ● In both counties and boroughs, the right to vote was extended to a greater number of men, although the value of property they owned or rented still determined who could vote.	● Still no secret ballot; bribery and corruption continued. ● Many boroughs with very small electorates survived. ● Most working-class men were still not able to vote; no women could vote. ● MPs were still unpaid, and therefore still tended to be wealthy landowners. ● The increase in the size of the electorate was small – from about 5% to $7\frac{1}{2}\%$ of the population. Rural areas still had a higher proportion of MPs than urban, industrial areas.

Source G

Power is transferred from one class of society, the gentlemen of England, to another class of society, the shopkeepers.

(The Duke of Wellington)

Source H

I support this measure, because I am sure that it is our best security against a revolution. I support this measure as a measure of reform; but I support it still more as a measure of conservation.

(Thomas (later Lord) Macaulay, speaking in a debate on the Reform Bill. He was then MP for the rotten borough of Calne)

Source I

The Whigs know that the old system could not last, and desiring to establish another as like it as possible, they drew up the Act in the hope of drawing together the aristocrats and gentry with a large reinforcement of the middle class.

(*The Poor Man's Guardian*, a radical newspaper)

The Duke of Wellington led the British army at Waterloo in 1815. He was Prime Minister from 1828 to 1830, and again in 1834. Many politicians like Wellington believed that the British parliamentary system was the ideal form of government.

PEOPLE IN THE PAST:
THE 1832 REFORM ACT

1 What did people think about the political system by 1832?
2 Why did people disagree about whether there should be political reforms?
3 Why was the 1832 Reform Act passed?
4 Cobbet (Source E) refers to a 'mighty revolution'. *The Leeds Mercury* (Source F) refers to 'The Victory of the People'. Judging from the evidence you have studied, would you agree with them?

🔆 Chartism

The 1832 Reform Act did not extend the right to vote very far. Parliament was still dominated by wealthy landowners. Many ordinary people wanted to see greater changes. Some joined the Chartist movement, which campaigned for further reforms. Why did people decide to join – or not to join – the Chartists?

Chartism got its name from The People's Charter, drawn up by William Lovett in 1838. It contained 'Six Points' (on the right).

Chartist methods

Chartism was never a really unified movement. Its two main leaders, William Lovett and Feargus

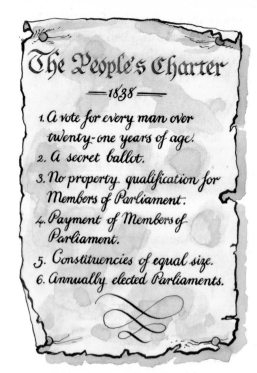

The People's Charter
—1838—
1. A vote for every man over twenty-one years of age.
2. A secret ballot.
3. No property qualification for Members of Parliament.
4. Payment of Members of Parliament.
5. Constituencies of equal size.
6. Annually elected Parliaments.

The Newport Rising, 1839

O'Connor, had very different ideas. Lovett was opposed to the use of force, while O'Connor was prepared to use force if necessary. There were a number of violent events associated with Chartism, the most serious occurring in Newport, Wales, in 1839. Thousands of miners marched into the town to try to release a Chartist leader from prison. Troops had been assembled in the town, and about 30 people were killed.

In August 1839, the Chartists tried to call a general strike – the 'Sacred Month' – but had to call it off due to lack of support. In 1842, 'Plug Riots' broke out in factories in Lancashire and Yorkshire. Workers removed plugs from steam boilers, stopping steam-powered machines from working.

Not all Chartist methods were violent. O'Connor's newspaper, the Leeds based *Northern Star*, carried powerful articles calling for political and social reform. Lovett called for greater educational opportunities to be given to working people.

O'Connor also set up the Chartist Land Company to buy up land, where workers could escape from the horrors of factory towns and support themselves by farming. He was not a good businessman, and the company collapsed in 1852.

The Chartists sent three petitions to Parliament, in 1839, 1842 and 1848, calling on the government to introduce the Six Points. Each one was rejected. The Chartists claimed the third one had over 5 million signatures. MPs were not so sure:

A Chartist demonstration at Kennington Common in London in April 1848

Upon the most careful examination, the number of signatures has been ascertained to be 1,975,496. It is further evident that on numerous consecutive sheets the signatures are in one and the same hand-writing. We have also observed the names of distinguished individuals attached to the petition, who can hardly be expected to agree with it – Her Majesty Queen Victoria, the Duke of Wellington, Sir Robert Peel, etc. We have also observed a number of names which are obviously fictitious, such as 'No Cheese', 'Pug Nose' and 'Flat Nose'.

(*Hansard*, the official report of proceedings in Parliament, 1849)

Political movements are often linked with the economic situation at the time. Chartist activity was at its height in the late 1830s and early 1840s, when there was a run of bad harvests and a recession in the textile industry. It decreased during the mid-1840s, when trade and wages began to recover, and peaked again in the late 1840s, following more bad harvests and another recession. Chartism virtually disappeared during the 1850s – a time of economic growth and rising wages.

Pushing the Charter into Parliament – a contemporary cartoon

CAUSES AND CONSEQUENCES: WHY DID PEOPLE JOIN THE CHARTISTS?

1 Look at The People's Charter. Explain why you think Chartists thought each of the Six Points was necessary.

2 Make a list of the different methods used by the Chartists to achieve their aims. Can you suggest any reasons why Chartism was unsuccessful in achieving its aims at that time?

3 Put yourself in the position of a skilled worker in the late 1840s. You are literate, and have an interest in politics. Would you join the Chartists or not? What factors would influence your decision?

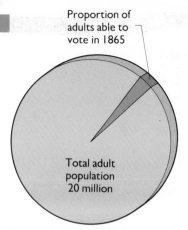

Proportion of
adults able to
vote in 1865

Total adult
population
20 million

The pie chart shows the proportion of people able to vote in 1865, compared with the total adult population

▦▦ Further Parliamentary Reform

During the 1850s and 1860s, Britain went through a period of growing prosperity. There was little political unrest. However, it became clearer that an expanding industrial and commercial country could not be controlled solely by a small group of landowners. In 1865, only 1,430,000 people could vote; the adult population was over 20 million. Pressure for reform continued to grow and, gradually, important changes were introduced.

Political caricatures of Gladstone (above) and Disraeli (below)

	Main terms of the act	Results of the Act
1867 Reform Act	In boroughs, the vote was given to all householders, and those who rented property above a certain value.	Many working-class men ('artisans') in towns could now vote.
	In the counties, however, the vote was only given to quite prosperous farmers and tenants.	Agricultural labourers still unable to vote.
	More seats were taken away from small boroughs and given to industrial centres.	Meant a fairer distribution of seats to more densely populated areas.
1872 Ballot Act	All voting was to be done in secret.	Voters could no longer be bribed or intimidated.
1884 Reform Act	Gave the vote to householders and lodgers in counties as well as boroughs.	Agricultural labourers could now vote.

William Gladstone (far left), Liberal Prime Minister 1868–74, 1880–1885, 1886, and 1892–94. His governments introduced important social reforms.

Benjamin Disraeli (left), Gladstone's chief opponent as leader of the Conservative Party after 1868. Prime Minister in 1868, and again from 1874–80. As well as introducing public health reforms, his government gave important rights to trade unions.

NEW POLITICAL CHATECHISM
WITH EMENDATIONS AND CORRECTIONS BY "TRUTH."

Granted that the Expenditure of the Liberals in 1861 was £73,000,000, what was it in 1865-£66,000,000

What was the Income Tax when the Liberals took Office in 1861 ? - - - - - - 10d. in the £

What was it in 1865 when they left Office ? - - - - - - - - 4d. in the £

What is it now under Tory management ? - - - - - - - - - 6d. in the £

Who are the men that proposed to charter a Roman Catholic University in Ireland by a } - **THE TORIES**
further grant of Money ? - - - - - - - - - - -

Who are they that seek to perpetuate an injustice like the Irish Church - - - **THE TORIES**

Who opposed the admission of Dissenters to the Universities ? - - - - - **THE TORIES**

Who abolished the Compound Rating Clause, thus compelling personal payment of Rates ? - **THE TORIES**

Who gave the Nation a uniform Penny Postage ? - - - - - - - **THE LIBERALS**

Who reduced the National Debt £12,000,000 ? - - - - - - - **THE LIBERALS**

Who reduced the Duties on Sugar, Wine, and Hops ? - - - - - **THE LIBERALS**

Who reduced the Duty on Coffee from 6d. to 3d. per lb. ? - - - - - **THE LIBERALS**

Who repealed the Duties on Soap, Bricks, Timber and Paper ? - - - - **THE LIBERALS**

Who amended and improved the so far good, but still imperfect, measure of Reform, } - **THE LIBERALS**
and carried it too ? - - - - - - - - - - - -

From these facts and many others, which could be quoted, it must be clear to all, } - **THE LIBERALS**
that the true friends of the Country are - - - - - - -

And to them only can we look for any reduction of Taxation, or removal of Burdens from the People.

☞ Electors ! ponder on these things, talk them over amongst yourselves when you meet together, and by your own firesides, and you must come to the conclusion that the Conservatives are not the men you ought to support, but THE LIBERALS !

Source J

An election poster, 1868

Although these reforms extended the right to vote, even after 1884 only about 30 per cent of the adult population could vote. However, both of the main political parties, the Conservatives and Liberals, now realised that they had to win the votes of the new voters. They began to offer new policies in the fight to win elections. They also had to make sure they put some of these policies into practice if they were to keep voters' support. As a result, a number of important social reforms were introduced by Conservative and Liberal governments, particularly after 1870. The 1870 Education Act laid the basis for a state education system. The 1875 Public Health Act improved sewerage, drainage and water supply. In the same year, the Artisans' Dwellings Act gave town authorities the right to clear slum dwellings.

Source K

A poster put up in a ship-builder's yard at the time of the 1868 Election

THE EFFECTS OF PARLIAMENTARY REFORM

1 Look at Source K. Note the date of the poster. Which employees might now be able to vote?

2 a Why was such a poster necessary at the time?
  b Would such a poster have been needed after 1872? Give reasons for your answer.

3 Look at Source J.
  a Which party do you think published the poster?
  b What arguments did this party use to persuade electors to vote for them?

4 Political posters are a form of propaganda. Does this mean that they are not reliable evidence?

5 Which large group of adults was still not allowed to vote, even after the 1884 Reform Act?

6 Why do you think the reforms you have studied were so slow to be introduced?

7 Do you think that these political changes helped to improve people's lives? Explain your answer.

Now refer back to your original chart. Is there anything you need to change?

Parliamentary reform was one way to improve people's lives and conditions. Another way was through the growth of trade unions. You will now investigate the development of unions between 1750 and 1900. Did they help ordinary people improve their working conditions during this period?

Early trade unions

In the late 1700s, workers often joined together in 'combinations' to protect themselves against employers, usually by going on strike. However, once the dispute had been settled, the 'combination' broke up. 'Trade clubs' also existed for skilled workers, like carpenters, tailors and shoemakers. They charged high subscriptions and provided sickness, old age and funeral benefits for their members. In 1799 and 1800, during the French Revolutionary Wars, the government, suspicious of any groups they thought might be potentially dangerous, passed the Combination Acts, which banned trade union activity. The Acts were not repealed until 1825.

The Feltmakers union card

The Felt Makers Company were First Incorporated in London, 1604.

THE ASSOCIATED FELT MAKERS OF THE UNITED KINGDOM OF GREAT BRITAIN AND IRELAND

WE ASSIST EACH OTHER IN TIME OF NEED.

The Tolpuddle Martyrs

After 1825, there were attempts to set up *national* trade unions. The most ambitious, the Grand National Consolidated Trade Union, was set up by Robert Owen in 1834. It soon claimed a membership of half a million, although very few members actually paid a subscription. The government was still opposed to unions. It persuaded magistrates in Dorset to bring to trial six farm labourers from the village of Tolpuddle. They had formed a union after their wages had been cut from 9s (45p) a week to 6s (30p). As was common at the time, they swore a secret oath of loyalty to the union. Because it was not actually illegal to belong to a union, they were charged under the Illegal Oaths Act, introduced in 1797 to use against mutineers in the navy! The Tolpuddle men were found guilty, and sentenced to seven years' transportation to Australia. After a public outcry, they were pardoned after serving two years.

'New Model' unions

There was little trade union activity during the rest of the 1830s and 1840s. Many working people devoted their energies to Chartism, which seemed to offer a better chance of improving their lives. However, in 1851, a new type of union, the Amalgamated Society of Engineers (ASE) was started. Members of the ASE had to pay a high subscription fee of 1 shilling (5p) a week. They could usually afford it. A skilled engineer could earn up to £2.00 a week, and they were in high demand during the 1850s. By the early 1860s, the ASE had over 30,000 members. The success of the ASE led to the setting-up of other unions for skilled workers. In 1868, the Trades Union

Congress (TUC) was set up to co-ordinate the activities of the unions. The government accepted these 'New Model' unions. It passed a series of laws in the 1870s which gave more legal protection to trade unions.

New unionism

'New Model' unions were for skilled, usually well-paid workers. Attempts to form unions for semi- and unskilled workers began in the 1870s. Some, like the National Agricultural Labourers' Union, set up by Joseph Arch in 1872, met opposition from employers, and failed. Other unions grew as a result of major strikes, such as the gasworkers' and dockers' strikes in 1889. The gasworkers won a reduction in their working hours from twelve to eight hours a day. The dockers gained a minimum wage of sixpence (2.5p) an hour — the 'docker's tanner'. By 1900, over two million workers were members of trade unions. However, employers often ignored the unions, and used 'blackleg' labour to break strikes. There were also legal problems facing unions: for example, unions could be held liable to pay damages to employers if their picketing prevented the use of blacklegs during strikes.

A membership card for the Amalgamated Society of Engineers

THE AMALGAMATED SOCIETY OF ENGINEERS

1 Look carefully at the ASE membership card. What do you think the following details are meant to show:
   a the two kneeling figures?
   b the two engineers on either side of the angel?
   c the dove above the angel?
   d the motto at the bottom of the picture?
   e the six scenes of workshops?
2 'The ASE was a moderate union, which rarely called its members out on strike.' How is this view supported by the membership card?

HOW SUCCESSFUL WERE TRADE UNIONS?

1 Draw a timeline to show the development of trade unions from 1750 to 1900.
2 a When were trade unions least active and effective?
   b What might explain this?
3 The 'New Model' unions were the first successful trade unions. Can you suggest why they were more successful than earlier unions?
4 What problems still faced the trade union movement by 1900?
5 Was trade unionism stronger in 1900 than it had been in 1750? Explain your answer.

Now refer back to your original chart. Do you need to change anything?

■■■ Women's rights

Most aspects of life in Britain between 1750 and 1900 appear to have been dominated by men. What about women? How far had their rights and opportunities improved by 1900?

Legal and political rights

For most of the eighteenth and nineteenth centuries, women had fewer legal rights than men. This slowly improved after 1839.

Source L

1839   Custody of Infants Act – gave more rights to divorced women to see their children, although the father still had almost complete control.

1847   Factory Act – women in textile factories were to work no more than 10 hours a day.

1857   Divorce Act – husbands could divorce their wives on the grounds of adultery (although women could not divorce for the same reason until 1923).

1870   Married Women's Property Act – allowed women to keep £200 of their own earnings. Previously, a husband owned all a wife's money and belongings.

1870   Women allowed to vote in elections to School Boards.

1871   Women were first admitted to Cambridge University (although were not allowed the same degrees as men until 1949).

1873   All women were allowed to see their children if they got divorced.

1877   Sophia Jex Blake became first woman doctor allowed to practise.

1884   Women were no longer considered a 'chattel' (possession) of their husbands.

1884   Third Reform Act – entitled about five million men to vote in elections to Parliament, but no women.

1888   Match girls' strike. Women workers at Bryant and May's match factory gained better pay and conditions.

1888   Women allowed to vote in local council elections.

Women strikers at the Bryant and May match-works, 1888. Their strike, publicised by a feminist journalist, Annie Besant, gained widespread support.

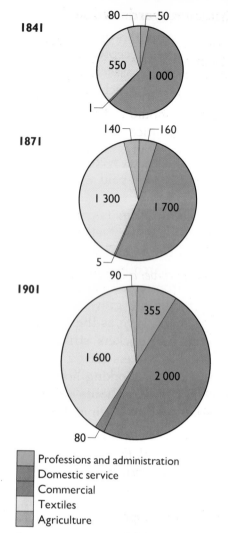

1841

1871

1901

- Professions and administration
- Domestic service
- Commercial
- Textiles
- Agriculture

Source N

The charts show changing trends in women's occupations between 1841 and 1901. The figures are in thousands.

Women and the right to vote

Many women felt that their position in society could only improve if they had the right to vote (*suffrage*) on equal terms with men. In the 1860s, a number of small organisations were established by women in major cities to campaign for the vote. The National Union of Women's Suffrage Societies (NUWSS) was set up in 1897. Its first president was Mrs Millicent Garret Fawcett. The NUWSS tried to co-ordinate the activities of the suffrage societies, by collecting petitions and trying to win support from MPs for the right to vote. However, by 1900, 'Votes for Women' appeared no nearer.

Source M: A comparison of men's and women's wages		
Occupation	**Men's average wage**	**Women's average wage**
Thimble-makers (1851)	75p–£1.05 a week	35–45p a week
Surface workers at tin-mines (1880s)	10p a day	5p a day
Tailoring machinists (1880s)	£1.12 a week	55p a week
Office workers (1880s)	£2+ a week	£1 a week
Carpet weavers (1890s)	£1.75 a week	£1 a week

Attitudes towards women

One reason that so little progress had been made towards gaining equal employment and political rights was because many people felt that women should not become involved in political life and the world of work, but should concentrate on their duties as wives and mothers.

William Thackeray, the novelist, writing in the 1850s, regarded a wife as:

An exquisite slave: a humble, flattering, tea-making, pianoforte-playing being, who laughs at our jokes, however old they may be; coaxes us and fondly lies to us throughout life.

Men were regarded as superior to women – even by scientists such as Thomas Huxley, writing in 1851:

In every excellent characteristic, whether mental or physical, the average woman is inferior to the average man. Even in physical beauty the man is superior.

Many women appear to have accepted their position in life throughout this period. Some did not. One of the first to challenge the situation was Mary Wollstonecraft, in 1792, in *A Vindication of the Rights of Women*:

I do not wish women to have power over men; but over themselves.

Father tells a story. What impression do you get of middle-class women from this picture?

However, other women were perhaps more influenced by the views expressed by Queen Victoria in a letter to Sir Theodore Martin, written on 29 May 1870:

The Queen is most anxious to enlist every one who can speak or write to join in checking this mad, wicked folly of 'Woman's Rights', with all its attendant horrors, on which her poor feeble sex is bent, forgetting every sense of womanly feeling and propriety. It is a subject which makes the Queen so furious that she cannot contain herself. God created men and women different – then let them remain each in their own position.

Mary Seacole was a Jamaican-born nurse who cured many cholera victims and gave medical attention to soldiers on both sides (Russian and British) during the Crimean War. She was a famous woman at the time, but her achievements have been overshadowed by those of Florence Nightingale.

HAD WOMEN'S LIVES IMPROVED BY 1900?

1 Study Source L.
   a What were the main legal rights gained by women between 1839 and 1888?
   b In what ways were they still denied rights that men had?
2 Study Source M. Did wages appear to improve for women workers between 1851 and the 1890s?
3 Study Source N. Did employment opportunities improve for women between 1841 and 1901?
4 What do you think were the major obstacles which prevented women from achieving equality with men?
5 By 1900 some women were talking about using violence to win the vote.
   a What might be the advantages and disadvantages of using violent methods?
   b Would you have joined this new women's movement? Give reasons for your answer.
6 'Women's lives improved a great deal between 1750 and 1900.' Judging from all of the evidence on this page, how far would you agree with this statement?

Ireland

For most of the period between 1750 and 1900, the whole of Ireland was part of the United Kingdom. Most Irish people were Roman Catholics, and resented the fact that much of Ireland's wealth and land was controlled by a minority of Protestant landowners with strong English connections. During the French Revolutionary Wars (1793–1815), the British government feared that the Irish might co-operate with the French in an invasion of England. By the Act of Union, in 1801, Ireland became part of the United Kingdom. The Irish Parliament was closed down, and 100 Irish MPs were elected to the House of Commons in Westminster. However, Catholics were not allowed to vote or become MPs until 1829.

During the 1840s, a campaign to repeal the Act of Union swept Ireland, but ended when tragedy struck the country. Many of the Irish were very poor, and farming methods were inadequate to feed the growing population. Between 1845 and 1848, the failure of the potato crop (the main food of the Irish) led to widespread famine. A million died and a million and a half more emigrated, mostly to America.

Many Irish people blamed the English for the problems facing Ireland, and in 1858 the Fenian Society was founded. Its aim was to achieve an Irish republic totally independent of the United Kingdom, and they began a series of bombings and violent demonstrations in England. Some English politicians, especially the Liberal Prime Minister, Gladstone, were prepared to give Ireland 'Home Rule', but Parliament defeated his proposals in 1886 and 1893. The House of Lords, which contained many owners of land in Ireland, was never likely to agree to Home Rule, and by 1900, Ireland was still ruled from London.

Source O

Irish industry in 1845

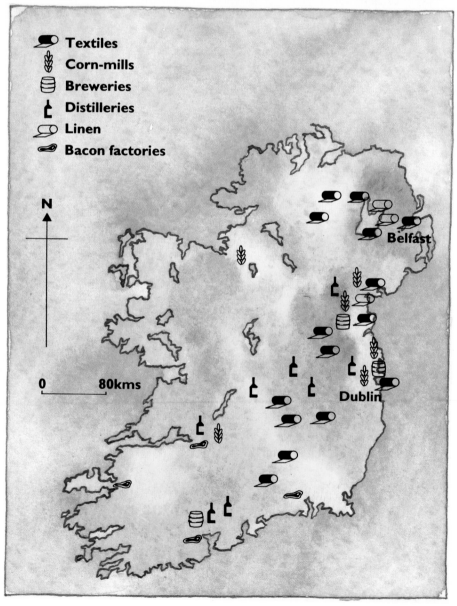

- 🗲 **Textiles**
- 🌾 **Corn-mills**
- 🛢 **Breweries**
- ⚱ **Distilleries**
- 👝 **Linen**
- 🥓 **Bacon factories**

N

0   80kms

Source P

We were soon among the most wretched habitations that I had yet seen. Many of them were flat-roofed hovels, half buried in the earth, or built up against the rocks, and covered with rotten straw, seaweed or turf. Seeing a cabin in a hollow, and surrounded by a moat of green filth, we found a single child about three years old lying on a kind of shelf and looking out of the door as if for its mother.

(Elihu Burritt, visiting the victims of the famine at Castlehaven, 1847)

EVIDENCE:
IRELAND IN THE 1840s

1 What does Source O tell us about Irish industry in 1845?
2 Which is the most useful source for finding out about Ireland in the 1840s? Explain your answer.
3 How useful are these sources in helping us find out about whether life for Irish people improved between 1750 and 1900?

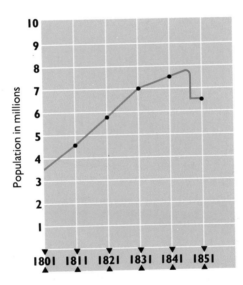

Source R
The effects of famine on the Irish population

Charles Parnell (1846–1891)
The Irish nationalist leader who wanted 'Home Rule' for Ireland

Summary: The effects of political change

In this chapter, you have been investigating the political changes which took place between 1750 and 1900. Had they helped to improve people's lives? Most historians would agree that they had. Political life was no longer dominated by the Crown and a few wealthy landowners. Although women were still not allowed to vote by 1900, most men over 21 could, and the main political parties had introduced reforms which improved people's working and living conditions. Trade unions were now legal, and had helped to improve pay and hours of work, sometimes through strike action. By 1900, the trade union movement had even set up its own political party, the Labour Party, to represent the interests of working people. However, poverty, ignorance, poor housing, ill-health and fear of unemployment were still widespread.

Having fun and learning more

Many of the changes you have investigated so far have been concerned with people's working lives. Changes also took place in the way people spent their leisure time, and in their ideas, beliefs and values. Developments in education, the arts, science and religion all played an important part in changing British life and society between 1750 and 1900.

This section looks at how people spent their leisure time. It is divided into two parts. The first one looks at the changes between 1750 and the mid-nineteenth century. The second part looks at how things had changed by 1900.

Source A

A horse-racing bill for Epsom, 1813

Source B

When the bets are made, one of the cocks is placed on either end of the stage; they are armed with silver spurs and immediately rush at each other and fight furiously. They rarely give up until one of them is dead. Sometimes a cock will be seen vanquishing his opponent and, thinking he is dead, jump on the body of the bird and crow noisily with triumph, when the fallen bird will unexpectedly revive and slay the victor. Of course, such cases are very rare, but their possibility makes the fight very exciting.

(Description of a cock-fight, mid-eighteenth century)

Source C

In cold weather you sometimes see a score of rascals in the streets kicking at a ball, and they will break panes of glass and smash the windows of coaches, and also knock you down without the slightest compunction; on the contrary, they will roar with laughter.

(An eighteenth-century description of a football match. Football was often played between two villages. The game began in one and ended in the other. Anyone who wished could join in)

Source D

A cricket match at Moulseyhurst in 1790

Source E

At the bear garden in Clerkenwell Green

These are to give Notice to all gentlemen and Gamesters, that this present Monday, there will be a match fought by four Dogs at the Bull. And a bull let loose to be baited with fireworks all over him and Dogs after him. With other Variety of Bull Baiting, Being a general day of Sport by all the Old Gamesters.

(A mid-eighteenth century advertisement for 'bull-baiting')

Source F

The operative population of Manchester enjoys little or no leisure during the week, the whole available time being absorbed by their occupations. The few hours which intervene between labour and sleep are generally spent at the tavern, or in making some necessary family arrangement.

(Letter from Dr Kay, 1833. Kay was writing to the Chairman of a Government Committee investigating leisure facilities)

Source G

No manufacturing town in England is worse situated for public or healthful recreation than Sheffield. Thirty years ago it had numbers of places as common land where youths and men could have taken exercise at cricket, quoits, football, and other exercises. Scarce a foot of all these common wastes remain for the enjoyment of the industrial classes.

(John Wardle, a Sheffield cutler, 1843)

Source H

Fifteen or twenty years ago the most barbarous kinds of sports were practised by the men such as bull baiting, dog fighting, cock fighting etc. These have died away and are now practised upon a very limited scale.

(A comment on changes in sport, c.1830)

Source I

'Miss Wicket and Miss Trigger'. A late eighteenth-century print.

Source J

Leisure Habits for Rich and Poor 1750-1850

Rich
- NOVEMBER-JANUARY WINTERING ABROAD
- FEBRUARY-APRIL COUNTRY HOUSE AND HUNTING
- MAY-JULY LONDON SEASON - BALLS AND OPERA
- AUGUST- COUNTRY HOUSE OR 'SELECT' SEASIDE RESORT
- SEPT-OCT COUNTRY HOUSE - SHOOTING

Poor
- 300 WORKING DAYS
- SMITHS IRON WORKS
- 52 SUNDAYS - but little to do.
- 10 (unpaid) 'HOLIDAY' DAYS - but nowhere to go.

Source L

Among the many changes which the latter half of this century has witnessed, nothing has been more typical of the new order of things than the active participation of women in its sports and pastimes. Lawn tennis must claim a large share of the responsibility for this.

(Herbert Chipp, the first secretary of the Lawn Tennis Association, writing in the late nineteenth century)

Source K

Tennis players, 1885

Source M

Some combined play by the Etonian forwards enabled them to approach the Rovers' goal, but they were speedily driven back. Macauley subsequently made a better attempt to score, while when Duckworth a few seconds later gave Douglas an opportunity he shot the leather over the bar of the Etonian citadel. As the time for play gradually shortened, the supporters of the Rovers became less confident, and there were shouts from the grand stand of 'Play up Blackburn', to which admirers of their opponents responded by cries of 'E-e-ton'.

(From a description of the 1882 FA Cup Final in the *Blackburn Times*. The match, between Eton and Blackburn Rovers, was held at Kennington Oval, and was won by Eton, their team composed of amateur 'Old Etonians'. However, Blackburn Rovers, a professional club, dominated football during the next decade. The Football League was formed in 1882, with 12 clubs, including Notts County, Preston North End, Blackburn Rovers, Stoke, Burnley and Accrington)

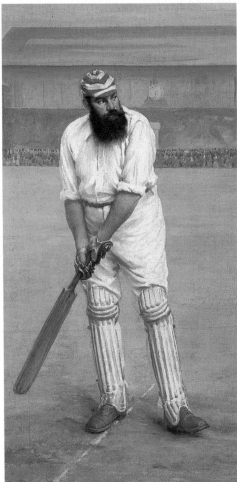

Source O

W. G. Grace who dominated English cricket from the 1860s to the end of the century

Source N

Drinking in a public bar in the late nineteenth century. This was a popular leisure time activity for the working classes.

Source R

Visitors to Blackpool

1851	2,200
1861	3,500
1871	7,000
1881	12,000
1891	21,000
1901	47,000

Source P

'Life at the Seaside (Ramsgate Sands)' by William Powell Frith, 1853–54

Source Q

There is a new dawn, a dawn of freedom, and it is brought about by the cycle. Free to wheel, free to spin out into the glorious countryside, unhampered by chaperon or, even more dispiriting, male admirer, the young girl of today can feel real independence of herself, and while she is building up her better constitution she is developing her better mind.

(A cycling enthusiast, Louise Jeye, 1895)

Source S

An advertisement for a phonograph, 1900

USING THE EVIDENCE: CHANGES IN LEISURE, 1750–1900

1 For each of the following, explain your answer carefully. Which sources suggest that some eighteenth-century sports:
   a involved gambling?
   b were bloodthirsty?
   c had different rules from modern ones?
   d involved women?
   e were changing by the early nineteenth century?

2 Which sources suggest that, for working people, there were fewer opportunities for sport and leisure activities by the 1840s?

3 What sources suggest that by the late nineteenth century:
   a mass spectator sports had become more common?
   b improvements in transport had changed some leisure activities?
   c some sports were organised on a national basis?
   d people were becoming more literate?
   e advances in technology had created new leisure activities?

4 Do these sources provide enough evidence to prove that changes in leisure activities benefited everybody between 1750 and 1900?

◷ Education

Changes in leisure activities were accompanied by changes in education. Education was not compulsory in 1750. There were no state schools, and although private schools existed, the quality of education was usually very poor. Were people better educated by 1900? Did education help to improve people's lives?

Schools for the rich

'Public schools', for the sons of the wealthy, survived throughout the period 1750 to 1900, and continued to provide the country with most of its political and military leaders. Conditions in them were often harsh and brutal. A riot at Winchester School in 1818 had to be put down by the army. Teachers were Church of England clergymen, and the curriculum was based on the study of classics – Latin and Greek.

Thomas Arnold, Headmaster at Rugby School from 1828 to 1842, introduced maths, geography and history into the curriculum, and

other public schools followed his example. Classics were still important, however, and most public schools tried to encourage a strong sense of Christian values and a 'team spirit', usually through competitive games.

Public schools for girls grew after 1850, when the North London Collegiate School was set up by Frances Buss. These followed a similar curriculum to boys' schools rather than teaching traditional female accomplishments like embroidery.

Schools for the poor

Schools for the poor were often set up by charities. They taught basic reading, writing and arithmetic ('The Three Rs'), and gave religious instruction. Two rival religious organisations, the British and Foreign Schools Society, and the National Society, set up hundreds of such schools across the country. However, many people felt that the poor should not become *too* educated.

Source A

My plan for instructing the poor is very limited and strict. They learn of weekdays such coarse work as may fit them for servants. I allow of no writing. My object has not been to teach opinions, but to form the lower class in habits of industry and virtue. To make good members of society has been my aim.

(Hannah More, a founder of the Sunday School movement, in 1789)

State involvement in education

In 1833, the government gave a grant of £20,000 to the two societies. This sum gradually increased, and inspectors were appointed to make sure the money was being spent wisely. Teacher training colleges were set up, and scholarships could be won by

Rugby being played at Rugby School in 1859, helping to foster a sense of 'team spirit'

promising pupil-teachers. By 1851, about a third of all children in England and Wales attended some type of school.

In 1862, the government introduced 'Payment by Results'. The size of grants to schools depended on pupils passing a series of tests, and on regular attendance.

The 1870 Education Act

By the late 1860s, British industry was being challenged by foreign competition, particularly from Germany and the USA. Many people believed that one reason for this was that education was much more widely available in Germany and America, where schools received government support and funding. In 1870, an Act was passed which allowed School Boards to be

PENNY WISE.

National Schoolmaster (going round with Government Inspector). "WILKINS, HOW DO YOU BRING SHILLINGS INTO PENCE?"
Pupil. " 'PLEASE, SIR, 'TAKES IT ROUND TO THE PUBLIC-'OUSE, SIR !! "

set up in areas where the voluntary society schools did not have enough places for all children. These School Boards, elected by rate-payers, could use public money to set up Board Schools. These were the first 'state' schools, although they did charge a small fee.

The government made elementary education compulsory up to the age of 10 in 1880, abolished fees in Board Schools in 1891, and raised the school leaving age to 12 in 1899. The curriculum began to broaden to include history, geography and practical subjects, but it was not until 1902 that the government decided to use public money for secondary education.

A London Board school, late 1800s

Source B

A visit by the school inspector, from the magazine *Punch*, 1873

Source C

Some of the tests from the 'Revised Code' of 1862, which introduced 'Payment by Results'

Arithmetic
Standard I   Form on blackboard or slate, from dictation, figures up to 20; name at sight figures up to 20; add and subtract figures up to 10, orally.
Standard II   A sum in simple addition or subtraction, and the multiplication table.
Standard III   A sum in any simple rule as far as short division (inclusive).
Standard IV   A sum in compound rules (money).
Standard V   A sum in compound rules (common weights and measures).
Standard VI   A sum in practice or bills of parcels.

EDUCATION FOR RICH AND POOR

1. What, according to Source A, was the main aim of education for the poor?
2. Which groups of people might have been opposed to the poor becoming *too* educated? Why?
3. From the evidence you have studied so far, what were the main differences between schools for the rich and poor? Were there any similarities?
4. Study Sources B and C.
   a. Can you think of any advantages of 'Payment by Results'?
   b. Can you think of any disadvantages?
5. Why do you think the government introduced the 1870 Education Act?
6. Do you think that people were better educated by 1900 than they had been in 1750?

Arts and science

MOST OF THIS BOOK HAS BEEN ABOUT THE ECONOMIC AND SOCIAL CHANGES IN BRITAIN BETWEEN 1750 AND 1900. THESE TWO PAGES ARE ABOUT SOME OF THE PEOPLE WHO HELPED TO CHANGE ART, ARCHITECTURE, LITERATURE, MUSIC, AND SCIENCE. DO YOU THINK THEIR WORK HELPED TO MAKE LIFE BETTER FOR ORDINARY PEOPLE BETWEEN 1750 AND 1900?

INK

CHARLES DICKENS (1812-1870)
- NOVELIST, WHO TACKLED SOCIAL PROBLEMS OF CRIME AND POVERTY IN NOVELS LIKE OLIVER TWIST AND GREAT EXPECTATIONS.

ALFRED, LORD TENNYSON (1809-92)
- POET, WHO REPRESENTED MANY OF THE PATRIOTIC, CHRISTIAN VALUES OF THE VICTORIAN UPPER CLASSES.
'INTO THE VALLEY OF DEATH RODE THE SIX HUNDRED.'

ROBERT BURNS (1759-1796)
- SCOTTISH POET, WHO WROTE ABOUT LOVE, NATURE, PATRIOTISM, AND THE PEASANT LIFE, OFTEN IN SCOTTISH DIALECT.
'WE'LL TAKE A CUP O' KINDNESS YET, FOR AULD LANG SYNE'

WILLIAM WORDSWORTH (1770-1850)
- POET, INSPIRED BY NATURE AND RURAL LIFE.
'I WANDERED LONELY AS A CLOUD THAT FLOATS ON HIGH O'ER VALES AND HILLS.'

SIR JOSEPH BANKS (1743-1820)
- A BOTANIST, WHO ACCOMPANIED COOK TO THE SOUTH PACIFIC AND GATHERED MANY SPECIMENS; HELPED TO FOUND KEW GARDENS.

ROBERT ADAM (1728-92)
- ARCHITECT, WHOSE STYLE WAS STRONGLY INFLUENCED BY THE STYLES OF ANCIENT GREECE AND ROME.

HOME SWEET HOME

JANE AUSTEN (1775-1819)
- ONE OF THE FIRST WIDELY-
- READ NOVELISTS. PRIDE AND PREJUDICE AND EMMA DESCRIBED THE LIVES OF THE RURAL MIDDLE AND UPPER CLASSES.

MICHAEL FARADAY (1791-1867)
- SCIENTIST, WHO DISCOVERED ELECTRO-MAGNETIC INDUCTION, THE BASIS OF ELECTRIC MOTORS.

GILBERT (1836-1911) and SULLIVAN (1842-1900)
- WROTE COMIC OPERAS SUCH AS THE PIRATES OF PENZANCE AND THE MIKADO.

JMW TURNER (1775-1851)
- PAINTER, WHO EXPERIMENTED WITH DIFFERENT TECHNIQUES TO CREATE NEW LIGHT AND COLOUR EFFECTS.

MARY SHELLEY (1797-1851)
- NOVELIST, BEST KNOWN FOR THE 'GOTHIC' NOVEL, FRANKENSTEIN.

Source D

Some of the pews for the rich were padded, lined, cushioned and supplied with every comfort. The poor, on the other hand, were seated on stools in the aisles; many of the seats were without backs, to prevent the occupants from falling asleep during the sermon, and the cold damp stone beneath their feet was the only place to kneel during prayer.

(J. Glyde, describing a church in Ipswich, 1850)

Source E

The rich man in his parlour
The poor man at his gate,
God made the low and mighty
And ordered their estate.

(A verse from the Victorian hymn, 'All Things Bright and Beautiful')

Source F

New churches built, 1801–50

Church of England	2,250
Non-conformist	39,200

Source G

Numbers of church worshippers, 1851

(approximate figures)

Total population of England and Wales	18,000,000
Number of possible worshippers (excluding young children, old people, invalids and Sunday workers)	12,500,000
Number of actual worshippers	7,250,000

Source H

Church attendance in major cities, 1882

Sheffield	23%
Liverpool	26%
Portsmouth	41%
Bath	52%

(National average: 37%)

Religion

People often say that religion was more important in the past than it is for most of us today. Religion was very important in the Middle Ages, and caused wars in the sixteenth and seventeenth centuries. Was religion still important between 1750 and 1900? Did religion help to improve people's lives?

Almost everybody in Britain in the eighteenth century regarded themselves as Christians, although there were different *denominations*, such as the Church of England, the Roman Catholic Church and the Quakers. The Church of England was by far the most important of these, and was the 'official', or 'established' Church. It was very wealthy, and senior clergy (archbishops and bishops) were men of great power and influence. The Church of England came under increasing criticism, however, for being 'out of touch' with the lives of ordinary working people, particularly in the growing industrial towns.

One reason why the Church of England was so influential was because a number of laws discriminated against members of other denominations. *Nonconformists* (Protestants who did not believe in the teachings of the Church of England) could not hold public office (for example, become Members of Parliament) until 1828; Roman Catholics could not even vote until after 1829. Despite this, however, the membership of other denominations grew.

Many people joined the Methodist movement, set up by John Wesley in the late 1730s. Originally a movement within the Church of England, Wesley set up a separate Methodist Church in 1784. He tried to make Christianity more attractive to working people, and travelled the country preaching until his death in 1791. Thousands flocked to hear him preach in open-air sermons, and Methodism became increasingly popular. By 1900, there were nearly half a million Methodists in Britain.

Wesley, the founder of the Methodists, preaching from his father's tomb

The Church and social reform

Some Christians played a major part in introducing social reforms. William Wilberforce led the campaign against slavery, and played a major part in persuading Parliament to abolish it throughout the British Empire in 1833. Elizabeth Fry, a Quaker, was active in prison reform between 1813 and her death in 1845, particularly in trying to improve the conditions of women prisoners. She believed punishment should not be for revenge, but to reduce crime and reform the criminal. Lord Shaftesbury tackled factory conditions and the exploitation of 'climbing boys', young boys who swept chimneys by having to climb up them.

In 1878, William Booth founded The Salvation Army. Its members wore a distinctive uniform, and held open-air meetings which mixed lively brass band music and preaching. The Salvation Army soon established a reputation for helping the poor, hungry and homeless.

Challenges to religion

Scientific discoveries during the nineteenth century encouraged some people to challenge traditional religious views. In 1859, Charles Darwin's *Origin of Species* caused a sensation by claiming that the human race was descended from apes rather than having been 'created' by God.

Charles Darwin (1809–1882)
A contemporary cartoonist's view

Salvation army women selling
goods made in their hostels

WAS RELIGION IMPORTANT?

1 Read Sources D and E. How could they help to explain the unpopularity of the Church of England at the time?
2 What do Sources F, G and H tell you about religion in the nineteenth century?
3 Do you think religion played a part in improving people's lives between 1750 and 1900?
4 One historian has written of the late nineteenth century: 'A lack of enthusiasm for religion affected all classes.' Can you *prove* this from the evidence in these pages?

Completing your investigation

The rise and fall of Great Britain

In 1750, most people in Britain lived in the countryside, and supported themselves by farming. Poverty was common, many people were illiterate, and transport and communication was difficult and slow. By 1900, the population had grown enormously. Millions of people lived and worked in towns and cities. Railways provided a cheap, fast form of travel, and most people were better educated, housed and fed. In the process, Britain had become the world's first and wealthiest industrial nation. However, by 1900, her position was being challenged. In this section, you will be looking at some of the reasons for Britain's growth – and decline.

Source A

The first industrial revolution occurred in Great Britain and is of particular interest in that it occurred spontaneously, without government assistance.

(Phyllis Deane, *The First Industrial Revolution*, 1979)

Source B

Britain's was the first industrialization of any national economy in the world. Even more remarkable, it occurred spontaneously, not being the result of conscious government policy sponsoring industrial progress.

(Peter Mathias, *The First Industrial Nation*, 1982)

Source C

In the eighteenth century, government encouraged trade by protection and by extending the country's colonial power.

(Howard Martin, *Britain Since 1700: The Rise of Industry*, 1988)

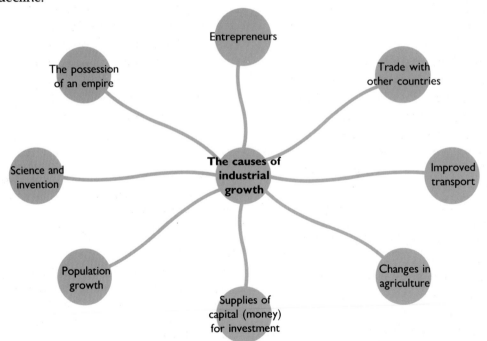

Entrepreneurs

The possession of an empire

Trade with other countries

Science and invention

The causes of industrial growth

Improved transport

Population growth

Supplies of capital (money) for investment

Changes in agriculture

DIFFERENT VIEWS: THE FIRST INDUSTRIAL NATION

1   Copy the diagram into your books. From what you have studied and learned so far, can you complete the diagram by adding reliable evidence which helps to explain how each point helped Britain to become an industrial nation?

2   Which do you think were the main reasons why Britain became an industrial nation? Explain your choice.

3   How do Sources A and B agree?

4   Source C seems to disagree with Sources A and B. What reasons can you suggest to explain this?

5   From what you have learned so far, do you think that Britain's industrial growth was planned by the government?

'All the world going to see the Great Exhibition' by George Cruikshank

In 1851, a 'Great Exhibition' was held at Hyde Park, in London. Housed in a huge glass structure, the 'Crystal Palace', the exhibition was designed to show off the tremendous industrial achievements which had been made by Britain. Although other countries' inventions and machines were also exhibited, there was little doubt that British trade and industry dominated the world.

Britain's main rivals in the second half of the nineteenth century, Germany and the United States, faced considerable problems in the years after the Great Exhibition. Germany was struggling for national unity; the USA was engaged in a disastrous civil war. In 1870, British trade was more than that of Germany, France and Italy put together, and was over three times greater than America's. By 1900, however, American and German industry had overtaken Britain. Both countries had been quick to use new manufacturing techniques – some of them, like the 'Open-Hearth' system of making steel, originally developed in Britain.

Source D
English overseers are trained too much to one thing or machine and do not adapt readily to circumstances.

(An American observer, writing in 1851)

Source E
There is a certain degree of timidity among English mechanics, resulting from traditional notions and attachment to old systems.

(James Nasmyth, the inventor of the steam hammer, 1854)

Source F
A hasty acceptance of apparent improvements is not to be welcomed. Because a machine has a large output, it does not follow that it must be better economically than one that produced less rapidly. Speed has to be paid for in one way or another.

(*The Engineer*, a British magazine, in 1901)

Source G
Britain, having changed so rapidly in the great transformation from the 1780s to the 1850s, showed less and less willingness to change in the late-nineteenth and twentieth centuries.

(Asa Briggs, *Iron Bridge to Crystal Palace*, 1979)

DIFFERENT VIEWS: THE WORKSHOP OF THE WORLD?

1 How do Sources D and E agree?
2 In what way does Source F seem to confirm the opinions in Sources D and E?
3 How do these sources help to explain why Britain had lost her industrial lead by 1900?
4 All four sources are statements of opinion. Does this mean they are not useful for historians?

⊜ Completing your hypothesis

As part of your investigation into British history between 1750 and 1900, you have been concentrating on two key questions.

⊙ *What changes took place?*
⊙ *Did these changes make people's lives better – or worse?*

You probably found it quite easy to see that very important changes took place as Britain became an industrial nation. It might have been more difficult to see whether these changes improved people's lives or not. Look back at your original hypothesis, and think about what you have studied so far. Which of the following statements would you agree with most?

a Life improved for everybody in Britain between 1750 and 1900.
b Life improved for most people in Britain between 1750 and 1900.
c Life improved for a few people in Britain between 1750 and 1900.
d Life got worse for most people in Britain between 1750 and 1900.

A Victorian family in the late nineteenth century

A Victorian family in the late nineteenth century

1 Write out the statement you have chosen.
2 Choose two of the characters below, or work in a group and choose one character each. Explain how, during their lifetimes, their lives might have:
   i improved;
   ii stayed the same;
   iii got worse.
   You can mention any of the following: working conditions; living conditions; clothing; transport; education; leisure; health; political rights, and any other areas you think are important.
   a **Robert Hardy** (1750–1807), an agricultural labourer in the Midlands.
   b **Sir Gilbert Brownlow** (1785–1856), a large landowner in Cambridgeshire.
   c **Elizabeth Jenkinson** (1790–1820), a pauper apprentice in a Lancashire spinning-mill.
   d **William Hall** (1795–1857), a handloom-weaver in Yorkshire.
   e **Kathleen Flaherty** (1820–73), a farm labourer's wife in Ireland.
   f **Charles Monkbridge** (1827–89), the owner of a steelworks in South Wales.
   g **Jane Townsley** (1830–1902), a wealthy widow living in London.
3 Do you need to change your hypothesis again?
4 Historians often disagree about whether there was an overall improvement in people's lives between 1750 and 1900. From what you have learned so far, can you suggest any reasons why?

How do we study history?

You have not just been learning about what happened between 1750 and 1900. You have been working like a historian – asking questions, suggesting answers or hypotheses and checking these first answers against evidence. You have also been learning more about the skills that historians need. You have been using sources as evidence. You have been investigating changes and continuity. You have been explaining the causes of events and developments.

HOW DO WE STUDY HISTORY?

1 Here are some statements that will help you to explain what you understand about the skills and ideas that historians use. Use examples from 1750 to 1900 to say why you agree or disagree with each statement.
   a **Change and Continuity**
      i Changes in working and living conditions always happened very quickly.
      ii Changes always help to improve people's lives.
   b **Causes and Consequences**
      i Political changes were caused by marches and demonstrations.
      ii The Industrial Revolution only affected people's working lives.
      iii A historian's task is just to list the causes and effects of an event.
   c **People in the Past**
      i Historians can study industries, politics and leisure separately because those topics did not affect each other.
      ii Factory workers had to slave in dirty, harsh and dangerous conditions.

2 **Different Views**
   Which of these reasons cause historians to disagree about the past? Explain the reasons for your choice.
   a Sources are not always clear in what they say and can be interpreted in different ways.
   b Historians' own attitudes and opinions make them disagree.
   c Events and ideas at the time historians are writing make them disagree.

3 **Evidence**
   a What kinds of sources tell us about Britain, 1750–1900?
   b Are written sources more useful for historians than pictures?
   c What questions should you ask about a source to check whether it is reliable?

1066

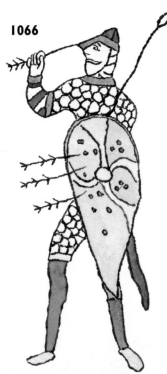

In the last three years you have studied the history of Britain since the Norman Conquest in 1066. These pages allow you to see and think about this whole stretch of history.

1 Choose the three events that you think were the most important. Explain why you chose them.
2 Choose three people who you think had the most impact on the people in Britain. Explain why you chose them.
3 Do you think that 1500 and 1750 were the right dates to divide up your study of British history?
4 List three things that have an important effect on your life that had not been invented by 1900.
5 If you had to live at a time before 1900 when would you choose and why?

The Triumph of Steam and Electricity

1215

1348-9

1475

1050	1100	1150	1200	1250	1300	1350	1400	1450

1066 Norman Conquest
1170 Murder of Becket
1199–1216 John
1215 Magna Carta
1272–1307 Edward I
1280s–1307 Conquest of Wales
Wars against Scotland
1327 Edward II deposed
1381 Peasants' Revolt
1413–22 Henry V

1066–87 William I
1086 Domesday Book
1154–89 Henry II
1189–92 Richard I's Crusade
1265 Beginnings of Parliament
1314 Battle of Bannockburn
1348-9 Black Death
1415 Agincourt
1475 Caxton introduced printing

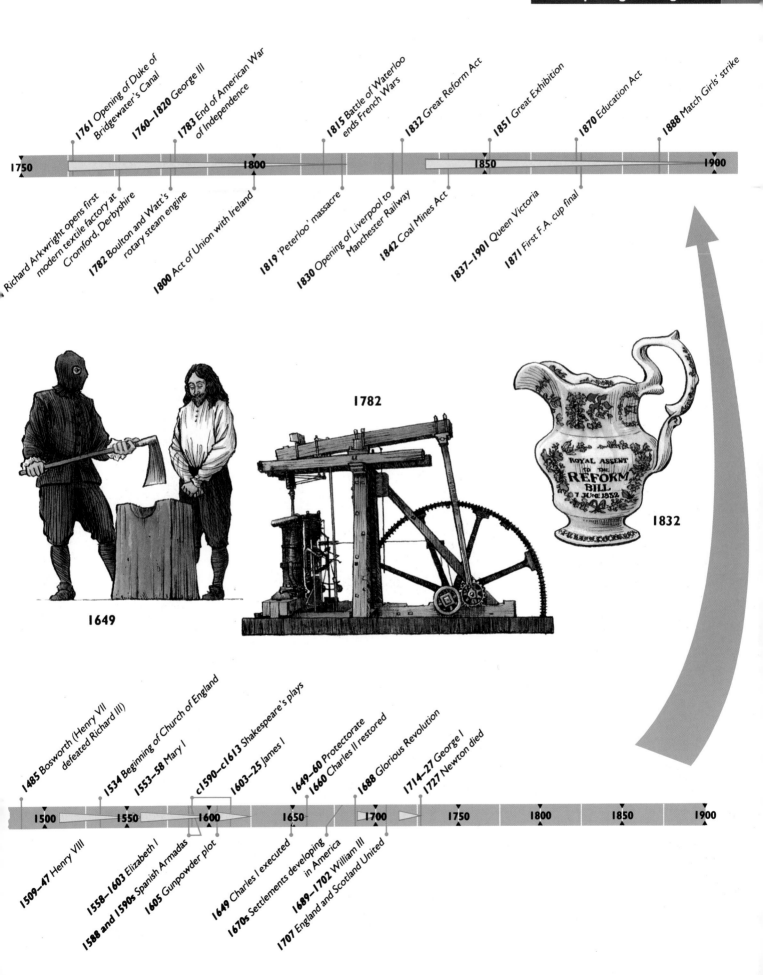

1761 Opening of Duke of Bridgewater's Canal
1760–1820 George III
1783 End of American War of Independence
1815 Battle of Waterloo ends French Wars
1832 Great Reform Act
1851 Great Exhibition
1870 Education Act
1888 Match Girls' strike

1750
1800
1850
1900

Richard Arkwright opens first modern textile factory at Cromford, Derbyshire
1782 Boulton and Watt's rotary steam engine
1800 Act of Union with Ireland
1819 'Peterloo' massacre
1830 Opening of Liverpool to Manchester Railway
1842 Coal Mines Act
1837–1901 Queen Victoria
1871 First F.A. cup final

1782

1649

1832

1485 Bosworth (Henry VII) defeated Richard III)
1534 Beginning of Church of England
1553–58 Mary I
c1590–c1613 Shakespeare's plays
1603–25 James I
1649–60 Protectorate
1660 Charles II restored
1688 Glorious Revolution
1714–27 George I
1727 Newton died

1500
1550
1600
1650
1700
1750
1800
1850
1900

1509–47 Henry VIII
1558–1603 Elizabeth I
1588 and 1590s Spanish Armadas
1605 Gunpowder plot
1649 Charles I executed
1670s Settlements developing in America
1689–1702 William III
1707 England and Scotland United

Index

▓ Acknowledgements

The publishers would like to thank the following for permission to reproduce photographs:

Page 3t & b Victoria & Albert Museum, London; p10t Cambridge University/Crown Copyright; p10t Mansell Collection br, bl Museum of English Rural Life, Reading; p11 Mansell Collection; p12c Mary Evans Picture Library; pp13tr, br & 15tr Mansell Collection; p16bl Bridgeman/British Library; p17 Science Museum, London; p18 bl Bridgeman/City of Bristol Museum & Art Gallery br Wedgwood Museum; pp19 & 20c Hulton Deutsch Collection, p20b E.T./National Museum of Labour History; p21 Cadbury Ltd; p24tl Metropolitan Museum, New York, c Mansell Collection, b Bridgeman/Cheltenham Art Galleries & Museums; p25t E.T. Archive, bl Bridgeman/United Services Club, br National Maritime Museum, London; p27t Victoria & Albert Museum, b Bridgeman/Christies; p28t Mansell Collection, b Mary Evans; p29tr Punch, c Mary Evans; p30cl E.T. Archive; pp31t & b, 32c & b Mary Evans; p33 British Library; p35 Mansell Collection; p36 National Portrait Gallery, London; p37 Mansell Collection; p38 Hulton Deutsch; p40 Mansell Collection; p41 Bridgeman/Victoria & Albert Museum; p42 Hulton Deutsch; p43 Illustrated London News; pp44tr & bl, 45tr & b, p46t Mansell Collection; pp46b & 48 Mary Evans; p49l National Portrait Gallery, r Mansell Collection; p50 British Library; p51 National Portrait Gallery; p52b E.T. Archive; p53 Bridgeman Art Library; pp54b, 55t & b, 56 bl, bc, br Mansell Collection; p56tr Bridgeman Art Library; p57b Hartlepool Museum Service; p58 Hulton Deutsch; p59 Bridgeman Art Library; p60c Mary Evans; p61t E.T. Archive, b National Library of Jamaica; p63t Illustrated London News, br Hulton Deutsch; p64t British Museum, c British Library, b Bridgeman/Marylebone Cricket Club; p65t British Museum; p66t & bl Bridgeman/Christopher Wood Gallery, br Bridgeman/MCC; p67t Royal Collection, St James's Palace, © H.M. The Queen, c Mansell Collection; p68 Rugby School; p69c Hulton Deutsch, tr Mansell Collection; p72 E.T. Archive; p73tr Mansell Collection, b Hulton Deutsch; pp75 & 76b Mansell Collection, p76t Hulton Deutsch; p78 Bridgeman/Guildhall Library, London.

Cover: Bridgeman/City of Bristol Museum & Art Gallery

Illustrations: Martin Cottam, Jeff Edwards, Mike Hingley, Martin Sanders, and Brian Walker